ROUTLEDGE LIBRARY EDITIONS: SOUTH AFRICA

Volume 13

SOUTH AFRICA
1906–1961

SOUTH AFRICA
1906–1961

The Price of Magnanimity

NICHOLAS MANSERGH

LONDON AND NEW YORK

First published in 1962 by George Allen & Unwin Ltd.

This edition first published in 2023
by Routledge
4 Park Square, Milton Park, Abingdon, Oxon OX14 4RN

and by Routledge
605 Third Avenue, New York, NY 10158

Routledge is an imprint of the Taylor & Francis Group, an informa business

© 1962 George Allen & Unwin Ltd

All rights reserved. No part of this book may be reprinted or reproduced or utilised in any form or by any electronic, mechanical, or other means, now known or hereafter invented, including photocopying and recording, or in any information storage or retrieval system, without permission in writing from the publishers.

Trademark notice: Product or corporate names may be trademarks or registered trademarks, and are used only for identification and explanation without intent to infringe.

British Library Cataloguing in Publication Data
A catalogue record for this book is available from the British Library

ISBN: 978-1-032-30347-5 (Set)
ISBN: 978-1-032-31183-8 (Volume 13) (hbk)
ISBN: 978-1-032-31186-9 (Volume 13) (pbk)
ISBN: 978-1-003-30849-2 (Volume 13) (ebk)

DOI: 10.4324/9781003308492

Publisher's Note
The publisher has gone to great lengths to ensure the quality of this reprint but points out that some imperfections in the original copies may be apparent.

Disclaimer
The publisher has made every effort to trace copyright holders and would welcome correspondence from those they have been unable to trace.

This is a reissue of a previously published book. The language is reflective of the time in which this book was published. In reissuing this book, no offence is intended by the Publishers to any reader.

SOUTH AFRICA 1906-1961
THE PRICE OF MAGNANIMITY

BY

NICHOLAS MANSERGH

M.A., D.Litt. (Oxon), Ph.D. (Cantab)
Smuts Professor of the History of the British Commonwealth
and Fellow of St John's College, Cambridge

with a Foreword by
Watson Kirkconnell
LL.D., D.Litt.

President, Acadia University

London
GEORGE ALLEN & UNWIN LTD
RUSKIN HOUSE MUSEUM STREET

FIRST PUBLISHED IN 1962

*This book is copyright under the Berne Convention.
Apart from any fair dealing for the purposes of private
study, research, criticism or review, as permitted under
the Copyright Act, 1956, no portion may be reproduced
by any process without written permission. Enquiries
should be addressed to the publisher.*

© *George Allen & Unwin Ltd., 1962*

PRINTED IN GREAT BRITAIN
in 11 point Fournier type
BY UNWIN BROTHERS LIMITED
WOKING AND LONDON

To Diana

FOREWORD

THE REID LECTURES were established in 1958 by Harvey T. Reid, BA (Acadia and Oxon), DCL (Acadia), of Saint Paul, Minnesota. Their purpose is to bring to Acadia University, at least every second year, some eminent scholar or man of affairs who will give a brief series of lectures on some important phase of history or political science. Their founder expressed a basic preference for some theme related to the British Commonwealth of Nations, but did not rigidly so restrict the lecturer.

Dr Reid was born in Hartland, NB, in 1891 and entered Acadia in 1908. On graduating in 1912, he was chosen as Rhodes Scholar for Nova Scotia and took an Oxford degree two years later. In the First World War, he served as a captain in the Royal Field Artillery and was wounded in action. In due time he became a member of the Minnesota State Bar Association and the American Bar Association. He has been president of the West Law Publishing Company since 1948 and of the American Law Book Publishing Company since 1952.

An invitation to deliver the first Reid Lectures was given early in 1958 to His Excellency Norman A. Robertson, Canadian Ambassador to the USA and formerly High Commissioner to the United Kingdom. His lectures were entitled 'Some Thoughts on the Commonwealth'. Charles Edmund Carrington, MA, Professor of British Commonwealth Relations in the Royal Institute of International Affairs, delivered the second series of lectures, in October 1959, on 'The Liquidation of the British Empire'. Nicholas Mansergh, the Smuts Professor of the History of the British Commonwealth in the University of Cambridge, delivered the third series of lectures at Acadia University in December 1960, and these lectures, somewhat expanded and extended so as to take account of South Africa's withdrawal from

SOUTH AFRICA 1906–1961

the Commonwealth on May 31, 1961, are reprinted here. The book starts with the 'magnanimous gesture' of 1906 by which the way was opened for a free Union between the predominantly British and the predominantly Boer provinces of South Africa. Professor Mansergh has clearly shown the good intentions of those who were principally responsible, but he concludes that the price of magnanimity has been high and has been paid for largely by the English-speaking minority and non-European majority in the Union.

WATSON KIRKCONNELL

President's Office
Acadia University
June 1961

CONTENTS

FOREWORD *page* 7

INTRODUCTION 11

I *The Magnanimous Gesture* 15

II *The Price for English-speaking South Africans* 38

III *The Price for Non-Europeans* 61

IV *Price and Reward* 89

INDEX 101

INTRODUCTION

There is an affinity between birth and death, between beginning and ending, so that when the second comes men's thoughts go back instinctively to the first. There is in this reason as well as a natural emotion. 'In my beginning is my end', wrote T. S. Eliot, and so much in the life of men and societies is determined in the circumstances of their birth that knowledge of the one is usually indispensable to an understanding of the other. Fifty-one years precisely elapsed between the inauguration of the Union of South Africa in its chosen capital of Pretoria on May 31, 1910, and its ending on May 31, 1961, when once more in a crowded capital a state new in constitutional form, the Republic of South Africa, was proclaimed. It is the purpose of this book to reconsider in the context of imperial and Commonwealth history the beginnings of the Union in the light of its ending. Since by a fortunate and nearly exact coincidence fifty years is the statutory period which has to elapse before British Government archives are open for examination, the ending of the Union in its original form falls at a time when British official papers on its beginnings have become available for study. I sought to take such advantage of this as was compatible with the scope and balance of this brief essay in historical and political analysis.

The problems of South Africa are problems that vex the mind and conscience of the mid-twentieth-century world. They are for that reason matters for debate in the market-place and at the United Nations; and the failure of successive South African Governments between 1948 and 1961 to make the least concession to the changing temper of the times has brought upon South Africa denunciations from the pulpit and from the press, boycotts, expulsion (for such in effect it was) from the Commonwealth, virtual isolation in the Western world, unrelenting criticism from newly independent Afro-Asian states, and the hostility of the Eastern Communist powers. It may be thought that where such controversy rages the historian can have little at least of immediate value to contribute and, therefore, had best remain silent. Yet is it not possible that, where indignation is stirred and passionate resentments aroused, the understanding that may come from viewing contemporary problems in longer perspective and the humility that must come from the study of the magnanimous actions and perhaps even more the errors of imaginative and enlightened men facing the selfsame problems in other days, may temper judgement, soften asperities and mark out the line of future progress? For it is at least certain that what is to come cannot be divorced in its turn from what is past. If in our beginning is our end so, too, as T. S. Eliot concluded his Second Quartet, in our end is our beginning.

. . . . .

I am much indebted to the staff of the Public Record Office and of the Commonwealth Relations Office and India Office Libraries for their courtesy and helpfulness. I have to thank the Trustees of the British Museum for giving me leave to consult the papers of Sir Henry Campbell-Bannerman and Mr Mark Bonham Carter for permission to use the Asquith papers in the Bodleian Library at Oxford. Evening conversations I am happy to remember with Professor E. A. Walker in the College Combination Room enlarged my understanding of topics dealt with in this book. My wife, to whom it is dedicated, gave me much help in my research and also prepared the index. My greatest debt is to the University of Acadia who invited me to deliver the Reid Lectures in December 1960 and in so doing encouraged me to elaborate South African themes which I had briefly outlined in a paper read at the XIth International Congress of Historical Sciences at Stockholm earlier in the year.

My Reid Lectures, somewhat extended in scope and time, are reprinted here. Looking out from the Acadia University Campus across the fertile Cornwallis Valley to Cape Blomidon and the

INTRODUCTION

sea it seemed not unfitting that by this long settled coastline of the oldest Dominion I should speak of the history, soon to be concluded, of another Dominion which in conception had owed much to Canadian example. Nearby, and offering a more personal link, was the birthplace and country home of Sir Robert Borden, Prime Minister of Canada and colleague of two of the principal architects of South African Union, General Botha and General Smuts, in the Imperial War Cabinet of 1917–18. They shared bright faith in the newly named British Commonwealth of Nations. It is unlikely that any of them foresaw and it is certain that none of them would have welcomed the ending of an association from which they hoped so much.

St John's College, Cambridge.   NICHOLAS MANSERGH
July 1961

I

THE MAGNANIMOUS GESTURE

> Has such a miracle of trust and magnanimity ever happened before?
> JAN CHRISTIAAN SMUTS

The South African War ended with the signature of the Treaty of Vereeniging on May 31, 1902. The eighth anniversary of this Treaty, May 31, 1910, was chosen by the delegates from the South African colonies in London in July 1909 for the inauguration of the Union of South Africa. It was a date which symbolized what they thought to be their great achievement—the reconciliation of victor and vanquished, Briton and Boer within a few years of the ending of a war that will always rank high in the annals of political folly, human endurance and stirring adventure and on the basis of that reconciliation the founding of a new South African nation as a Dominion of the British Crown. It seems not inappropriate now that their work in its imperial aspect at least is all undone, to reassess the nature of their achievement, its limitations in the light of British expectations and, most of all, its place in the history of the British Commonwealth. Hailed in 1910 as a great triumph of Liberal magnanimity and South African statesmanship, the Union was then thought to put a coping stone on the edifice of the self-governing Empire. With unification, said Lord Crewe, who piloted the South Africa Bill through the House of Lords, the Dominions might be thought of as being in something like their final form with 'the great American group, the great Pacific group and the great African group'.[1] When, however, the Prime Ministers of the

[1] House of Lords Debates, July 27, 1909, Vol. II, col. 767.

South Africa 1906–1961

Commonwealth met in London in May 1960 in the shadow of the shootings at Sharpeville[1] and on the eve of the fiftieth anniversary of Union—Philip Guedalla once commented on 'the ghastly ineptitude of anniversaries'—they let it be known that they were preoccupied with less sanguine reflections and that far from accepting South Africa as one of the chief supports of a Commonwealth wider and more embracing than Lord Crewe conceived, they were confronted with the question whether that Commonwealth might not be more securely united were South Africa excluded from it. They returned their answer to that question when they met again in March 1961 and on May 31st that year, the fifty-first anniversary of the Act of Union, South African membership ended in the interests of Commonwealth unity.

By the choice of the date for inauguration the act of Union is linked with the Treaty of Vereeniging. But there is another and intermediate date with which it is more appropriately to be associated in the history of the British Commonwealth—the date of the accession of the Liberal Government to office in December 1905. It was the decision of that Government to restore self-government to the defeated Boer republics which, immediately at least, opened the way to Union, and the imperial statesman whose name has been most nearly associated with the making of it was the Liberal Prime Minister, Sir Henry Campbell-Bannerman. A phrase he used—'methods of barbarism'—was thought by Botha to have left the door open for Anglo-Boer reconciliation after the war; a talk with General Smuts on February 7, 1906, in the opinion of Smuts, 'settled the future of South Africa';[2] a speech to the Cabinet on February 8, 1906, which Lloyd George was to describe as 'the most dramatic, the most

[1] On March 21st, sixty-seven Africans, demonstrating against the Pass Laws to which they were subjected, were shot by the South African police.
[2] S. G. Millin, *General Smuts* (London, Faber & Faber, 1936), Vol. I, p. 213.

THE MAGNANIMOUS GESTURE

important ten minutes' speech ever delivered in our time',[1] persuaded his colleagues that self-government for the defeated Dutch republics should be restored and moved one member of the Cabinet to tears; and if death in April 1908 deprived Campbell-Bannerman of the satisfaction of seeing the fulfilment of his South African policy two years later, nothing could deprive him among those of all men best qualified to judge of the reputation he had acquired as the chief architect of the South African settlement. To this none testified more movingly than General Botha who, when all was finally agreed in London in 1909, invited the Cabinet to dine with him. There were no speeches—only two toasts. After the health of the King had been drunk General Botha rose and only said, 'To the Memory of Sir Henry Campbell-Bannerman'.[2] Of how few can so little ever fittingly be spoken! The radical Scottish shipowner, thought by *The Times* to be the one weak spot in a ministry of many talents, has his niche secured in history by an act of magnanimity which opened the way to Union in South Africa and thereby enthroned, even in the fastnesses of the imperial tradition, notions of liberal enlightenment without which the British Empire might never have become a Commonwealth of Nations. Yet, by a strange paradox, now that transformation is well-nigh accomplished, there are growing doubts as to whether the policy that so profoundly influenced British thinking on imperial relations was in itself and at root either liberal or enlightened.

A Gesture and its Timing

The action which earned for Campbell-Bannerman so enviable a reputation for magnanimous statesmanship was the granting of

[1] Lord Riddell, *More Pages from My Diary* (London, Country Life, 1934), p. 144. Lloyd George told Sir Robert Ensor many years later that the Prime Minister's speech was 'so unanswerable as to secure at once the unanimous assent of his hearers, many of whom had till then held a different opinion'. See R. C. K. Ensor, *England 1870–1914* (Oxford University Press, 1936), p. 390, fn. 2.

[2] John, Viscount Morley, *Recollections* (London, Macmillan, 1917), Vol. II, p. 145.

responsible self-government first to the Transvaal on December 6, 1906, and then to the Orange River Colony (after Union, and to the great satisfaction of its inhabitants, known once more as the Orange Free State) on June 5, 1907, and it is well to enquire at the outset to what extent the adjective was merited. What had happened? And wherein lay the magnanimity? Two small trekker republics had been overwhelmed after a gallant struggle by the forces of an Empire in the plenitude of its power, their Governments overthrown, their territories absorbed within that Empire, their peoples compelled to become subjects of the British Crown, and then, after five years, domestic self-government had been restored to them. An act of retribution might seem a fitting description; Mr Macmillan on his return from his African tour some fifty-four years later, however, spoke of it as 'an act of unparalleled generosity'. In the context of twentieth-century international relations, but no other, this seems a just verdict.

The new constitutions were conferred by Letters Patent thereby avoiding certain repudiation by the Lords. In the Commons, the Leader of the Opposition, Mr A. J. Balfour, considered that the Government in restoring self-government to the Transvaal were attempting 'an experiment of the most dangerous description', and opined that 'no human being ever thought of such an experiment before—that of giving to a population equal to, and far more homogeneous than our own, absolute control of everything civil and military'.[1] It was, he concluded, in what was surely the most recklessly phrased utterance on imperial policy ever made by this 'father-figure' of the Statute of Westminster Commonwealth, 'the most reckless experiment ever tried in the development of a great colonial policy'.[2] Campbell-Bannerman, left with only one minute in which to reply to the assault of the Unionist Party and its leader, used it to say he had 'never, in the whole of his parliamentary

[1] House of Commons Debates, 4th series, 1906, Vol. CLXII, col. 801-2.
[2] *Ibid.*, col. 804.

career, listened to a more unworthy, provocative, and mischievous speech' than that of Mr Balfour, before clamour from the Opposition benches drowned his voice and filled the allotted time.[1]

The violence of Balfour's denunciation of Liberal policy derived from an expressed anxiety lest the Transvaal, given self-government, would make 'every preparation, constitutionally, quietly, without external interference, for a new war'.[2] This was a fear which Balfour himself may not have entertained overseriously and assuredly one which history has shown to have been ill-founded. But behind it lay a more reasonable and widespread misgiving lest the Liberal Government were acting with undue precipitation in South Africa. How carefully had they weighed the implications of their policy before deciding on it? Can it be said, for example, that the Liberal Government acted generously but without due consideration of the likely consequences of their action? These are questions of much importance on which judgement for the moment may best be deferred. But if one enquires further whether it can be maintained, as some would now have us believe, that the Liberal Government took action, as was said of a seventeenth-century Duc d'Orléans, like other men take a bath—they shut their eyes and jump in—then even at the outset some explicit judgement is possible.

The evidence, as supplemented by the recently opened files of the Colonial Office, provides a conclusive and for the Liberals a creditable answer to any suggestion that they acted on such blind or sudden impulse by making it abundantly, if disappointingly, clear that there was in fact no Damascus Road miracle about the conversion of the Cabinet in 1906, but rather a decision about timing, finally reached in the face of conflicting counsel and in dramatic circumstances, which none the less stemmed from Liberal thinking about South Africa in the long, lean years of

[1] J. A. Spender, *Life of the Right Hon. Sir Henry Campbell-Bannerman* (London, Hodder & Stoughton, 1923), Vol. II, p. 242.
[2] House of Commons Debates, 1906, Vol. CLXII, col. 802.

opposition.[1] That was why it was a decision which came as no surprise either to administrators in Whitehall to whom it was not generally welcome or the Boer leaders in the Transvaal to whom it was. After the Government's intention to grant full self-government to the Transvaal at the earliest possible date was made public, Lord Selborne reported from Johannesburg, on February 23, 1906, that it 'was not unexpected and has excited no opposition from any quarter'.[2] But to seek an answer to the earlier and more realistic questions posed above, it is essential to look back to the Liberal record, and more especially to that of its leader, in the war years and to consider the South African problem in the form in which it confronted the Liberal Cabinet on its accession to office in December 1905.

Lord Rosebery, who contributed much in his own idiosyncratic way to Liberal divisions during the South African War, spoke of the 'Liberal throne' as 'the most uneasy that had existed since the partition of Poland'.[3] The occupant of the throne, Campbell-Bannerman, was at once ill-fitted and little disposed in matters on which he felt strongly to conciliate either the Liberal Imperialist dissidents to the Right or the small body of radical pro-Boers to the Left. He never doubted that the war must lead to the annexation of the Boer republics. What concerned him was the sequel to annexation and he believed that that would turn upon the way in which the war was fought and peace was made. It was because he foresaw annexation and, with it, the prospect at last of Union that he was outraged when political considerations were sacrificed to so-called military necessity. Briton and Boer would have to live together after the war; it was therefore of the highest importance to create as little ill will as possible and, if we could, to 'make even the stern

[1] Cf. J. A. Spender and C. Asquith, *Life of Lord Oxford and Asquith* (London, Hutchinson, 1932), Vol. I, p. 179, for Asquith's views on the final peace settlement as a test of the distinction between Unionist and Liberal attitudes.

[2] Colonial Office Records at the Public Record Office (hereafter referred to as C.O.) 291/96.

[3] Quoted in Spender, *Campbell-Bannerman*, Vol. II, p. 2.

The Magnanimous Gesture

necessities of war minister to conciliation'. 'That,' he continued,[1] 'is why I have denounced and, heaven helping me, will continue to denounce, all this stupid policy of farm-burning, devastation, and the sweeping of women and children into camps.' But it was not, one suspects, reason alone that stirred him.

Miss Emily Hobhouse saw Campbell-Bannerman on the morning of June 13, 1901, and of all whom she sought out in her endeavours to expose the evils of concentration camps ineptly conceived and disastrously administered[2], he alone seemed to her 'to have the leisure and the determination to hear and understand everything. Indeed, he gave me so much scope that I was enabled to pour out to him more fully than to anyone else I met the detailed horrors of those camps. For nearly two hours he listened with rapt attention, now and then putting a question ... and now and again murmured *sotto voce* "methods of barbarism, methods of barbarism".'[3] The next day that phrase was uttered at the Holborn Banquet and the Liberal leader assailed with angry outbursts of patriotic denunciation. But he did not bow before the storm. On the contrary he held firmly to the opinion he had expressed, reserving for particular contempt Balfour's unhappy remark about the women and children in the camps, where the average death-rate was 116 per thousand, 'not having all the comforts we desire'.[4] At Stirling, on October 25th, unrepentant, Campbell-Bannerman repeated his now notorious phrase. 'The whole country in the two belligerent states outside the mining towns', he said, 'is a howling wilderness. The farms are burned, the country is wasted. The flocks

---

[1] At Peckham, August 7, 1901, quoted *ibid.*, p. 3.

[2] The maximum number in the camps was 117,871. Of these 20,117 died in the epidemics which swept through them.

[3] Letter from Miss Hobhouse to Lord Pentland, February 1913, quoted in G. B. Pyrah, *Imperial Policy and South Africa 1902–10* (Oxford at the Clarendon Press, 1955), p. 247. See also Spender, *Campbell-Bannerman*, Vol. I, p. 335, for another version and Campbell-Bannerman Papers, British Museum. Add. MS. 41243A, f. 36, for his own notes.

[4] See Campbell-Bannerman's 'notes and extracts for use in speeches'. Add. MS. 41243A, ff. 36, 37.

and herds are either butchered or driven off; the mills are destroyed, furniture and implements of agriculture are smashed. These things are what I have termed methods of barbarism. I adhere to the phrase. I cannot improve upon it. If these are not the methods of barbarism what methods did barbarism employ?'[1] And then he returned to the underlying theme of his South African policy, saying that after the assertion of British military authority the war should be brought to an end in an honourable way by impressing on their antagonists 'our ultimate and essential friendliness' to them.

'I never could have believed', said a Unionist leader of Campbell-Bannerman to John Morley some years later, 'that a man who had used that language could ever become Prime Minister of England.'[2] But Boer commandos in the Veldt, facing an end which neither skill nor courage could much longer avert, found an echo in their hearts. Years later Louis Botha told Campbell-Bannerman's biographer of 'the tremendous impression' which had been made upon men fighting a losing battle with an apparently hopeless future by the fact that the leader of one of the great English parties had had the courage to say this thing and to brave the obloquy which it brought upon him.[3] Far from encouraging the Boers to a hopeless resistance, as Campbell-Bannerman's critics alleged, it touched their hearts and, if Botha's testimony be accepted, made them think seriously of reconciliation. Three words, he said 'made peace and union in South Africa: "methods of barbarism".' At the very end, at

[1] Spender, *Campbell-Bannerman*, Vol. II, p. 9.

[2] Morley, *Recollections*, Vol. II, p. 141.

[3] Spender, *op. cit.*, Vol. I, p. 351. It is not surprising that Campbell-Bannerman's criticisms aroused passionate feeling in a country at war even though he was careful to direct them at those responsible for the conduct of operations and was warm in his praises of the British troops in South Africa. Yet how much better might be the prospects of peace in Europe today had some Russian leader expressed publicly criticisms of the methods employed by Russian forces in the suppression of the Hungarian revolt of 1956 and thereby opened the way to a restoration of self-government there five years later. Silence may have, and frequently has, its greater price.

The Magnanimous Gesture

Vereeniging, when not for the first or last time Smuts had concluded that Milner was 'impossible', Kitchener took him outside and gave it as his opinion that in two years' time a Liberal Government would be in power and that it would grant a constitution for South Africa. It was only an opinion but, said Smuts later, it 'accomplished the peace'.

When not two but three years later the Liberals came to power the Boers, however, were not without their doubts. Would pledges given in opposition be honoured? Were those pledges explicit in respect of the restoration of self-government? Above all was there not evidence that Campbell-Bannerman's leadership was in question and might he not be persuaded or compelled to exchange effective but exacting leadership in the Commons for indolent and impotent isolation in the Lords?[1] Should not the Boers, like the Irish, also reckon with the Liberals' well-known and 'eel-like powers of evasion'?[2] In the citadels of British power, as they had reason to know, they were not trusted.

In the Lyttelton constitution the outgoing Conservative administration had outlined their proposals for introducing an elective element into the government of the defeated Dutch republics. The Liberal Cabinet, on its accession to office, had to decide whether or not to proceed with those proposals. This was a matter of constitutional importance but even more was it a test of ultimate intention. The Lyttelton constitution provided for representative but not responsible government. Laws passed by the Assembly were to remain subject to the Governor's right

[1] It was Lady Campbell-Bannerman who inspired Campbell-Bannerman's resolve not to allow himself to be kicked upstairs. Lord Morley later said that by her action she had placed the nation in her debt. She had also placed the Boers in her debt. Since the services of wives usually pass unrecorded Morley did well to note that 'this must be added to the many historic cases where women have played a leading part in strengthening the counsels of ministers, sovereigns, great reformers, and even popes'. *Recollections*, Vol. II, pp. 142–3.

[2] The phrase was used by *The Freeman's Journal* and has been attributed to Tim Healy by Conor Cruise O'Brien in *Parnell and his Party* (Oxford, 1957), p. 164.

to reserve them and the Imperial Government's power to veto them. Executive authority was vested in the Executive Council, the members of which were responsible not to the Assembly but to the Governor and they alone might make fiscal recommendations. Article 7 of the Treaty of Vereeniging had promised to the defeated Boers representative institutions leading up to self-government as soon as circumstances allowed. The Lyttelton constitution was therefore wholly in line with the Treaty. Was it wise to go farther, to discount continuing Boer hostility, to give to the Boers in the Transvaal the opportunity, through control of the executive by a popularly-elected assembly in which they were likely to secure a majority, of winning back by the ballot box what they had lost in the war? Official opinion in the Colonial Office, which unlike Unionist opinion in Parliament could not be discounted as *parti pris*, was full of misgivings.

A Colonial Office paper, dated December 16, 1905, put to the Cabinet what was described as the 'main question'—namely as to whether a fair trial should be given to the Transvaal representative constitution or whether the Government preferred to adopt the alternative of an immediate grant of full self-government.[1] Colonial Office advice underlined the advantages of an intermediate stage—as did Lord Selborne, the Conservative successor to Milner as High Commissioner for South Africa and Governor of the Transvaal and the Orange River Colony, who alluded to the value of two or three years of representative government in the former republics as a 'transitory stage to responsible government'.[2] It was conceded that in neither colony did there seem to be any strong body of opinion in favour of representative government, the Het Volk and the Responsible Government parties in the Transvaal having joined forces on this issue to command a majority, while in the Orange River Colony the demand was for 'nothing less than responsible

[1] *Transvaal Constitution (Colonial Office Confidential Print), African (South) No. 796.* Subsequent references to these Confidential Prints will give the title *African*, followed by the number.

[2] Selborne to Elgin, January 13, 1906. C.O. 291/95.

The Magnanimous Gesture

Government'.[1] But despite this the predominant official view was fairly summarized in a minute by the Assistant Under-Secretary which read: 'Altogether, it seems that the question of conceding full self-government to either Colony is one which His Majesty's Government would do well to postpone for more mature consideration than can be given to it at a few hours' notice.'[2] Such, however, was not the opinion of the new parliamentary Under-Secretary of State for the Colonies, Mr W. S. Churchill. He argued in a forthright paper, dated January 2, 1906, that to proceed 'direct to Responsible Government would be only a more punctual and perfect fulfilment' of the Vereeniging agreement. More important the Imperial Government had abandoned one practical and defensible position with the substitution of representative for Crown Colony government. When one crest line has been abandoned, proceeded Mr Churchill, it is necessary to retire to the next. 'Halting at a "half-way house" midway in the valley is fatal.' What he feared from such a course was the extraction of self-government by pressure from the Transvaal and the Orange Free State. 'What we might have given with courage and distinction both at home and in South Africa, upon our own terms, in the hour of our strength, will be jerked and twisted from our hands—without grace of any kind—not perhaps without humiliation—at a time when the Government may be greatly weakened. . . .'[3] On January 19, 1906, and nearly three weeks before Smuts saw Campbell-Bannerman, A. B. Keith, then a clerk in the Colonial Office, minuted that he gathered that the question now was whether 'responsible government will be granted at once or whether the Representative Assembly will be allowed to sit (for

[1] 'Het Volk' (The People) was formed on the decision of a Congress held at Pretoria in May 1904. General Botha was the moving spirit and conciliation between Dutch and English with a view to forming a united nation was a principal aim of the party. The English-speaking Responsible Government Party was formed in the same year.

[2] December 17, 1905, signed F[rederick] G[raham]. Mr (later Sir Frederick) Graham was Assistant Under Secretary of State at the Colonial Office 1897–1907 (*African*, 796A). [3] *African*, 804.

a session) and pass the legislation establishing responsible government'.[1] On this the Assistant Under-Secretary (Mr Graham), a man who evidently had little liking for, and even less confidence in the Boers, commented that it would be better 'unless H.M. Government were prepared to resist' a demand for responsible government 'to give it at once on our own terms'.[2] 'It would be of course', he continued, 'without precedent but the circumstances are without precedent. Apart from the fact that the inhabitants of the Transvaal are—politically—mere children compared with those of the Canadian, Australian and other South African colonies when they got Responsible Government, this country which has spent two hundred million pounds and sacrificed many lives in acquiring the new colonies has a right to dictate its own terms in the grant of Rssponsible Government.'

The writer of this minute diagnosed critically but correctly the likely Cabinet response to the rising clamour and heightening expectation of responsible government in the Transvaal, for on January 30, 1906, a Cabinet Committee accepted the view that the advent of responsible government could not be delayed beyond 'the present year'.[3] Yet he gravely miscalculated in thinking of 'dictation' of 'our own terms'. The Liberal Government could act generously or not act; it could not act generously and dictate its own terms. The precedents of responsible self-government elsewhere and, in one most important particular, of the terms of the Treaty of Vereeniging saw to that. There had to be a gesture or nothing, as Mr Churchill found it easier to understand than civil servants.

General Smuts brought a memorandum[4] with him to London with arguments of a kind likely to appeal to the Liberal Cabinet and reinforce Mr Churchill's conclusions. The young Boer lawyer whose outstanding gifts as an undergraduate at Christ's

[1] C.O. 291/95. The writer was later well known as Professor Keith.
[2] *Ibid.*
[3] *African*, 815. See also letter from Elgin to Campbell-Bannerman dated January 23, 1906. Campbell-Bannerman Papers Add. MS. 41214, f. 39–40b.
[4] Reprinted in *African*, 837.

The Magnanimous Gesture

College, Cambridge, had not escaped the notice of the great F. W. Maitland[1] and who had acted as adviser to President Kruger in the Conference at Bloemfontein, the breakdown of which precipitated the outbreak of the South African War, well understood how to present his case. He was reassuring about Boer acceptance of the accomplished fact of annexation; he was encouraging in his allusions to Canadian precedents; he was astute, if also specious, in suggesting that 'the great practical issue in Transvaal politics, before which the racial issue has receded, is the distribution of political power as between the mine-owners and the permanent population of the land, English as well as Dutch'; and he was conclusive in respect of timing. 'There may be some danger', he wrote, 'in trusting the people too soon, but there may be much greater danger in trusting them too late.' In sum the immediate and unreserved application of Liberal principles by the Liberal Government to the defeated Dutch republics was his recommendation and he foretold that within five years of the grant of responsible self-government federation in South Africa would be a possibility.

Neither Smuts's person nor his case passed without critical comment. 'Mr Smuts', wrote the Assistant Under-Secretary at the Colonial Office,[2] 'is a Boer and a lawyer. His memorandum ... exhibits all the cunning of his race and calling.' But Campbell-Bannerman was more confident—or more confiding—and, needing little or no persuasion himself, persuaded his Cabinet to accept the arguments—not only from Smuts in their South African setting but, as we now see, from Churchill as well in an appropriate imperial context—for the immediate restoration of self-government. This was Campbell-Bannerman's decisive contribution. It is one easy to underestimate in retrospect.

The Cabinet of 1906 consisted of nineteen members and Haldane complained that this over-large body was like a meeting of delegates at which 'the powerful orator secured too much

---

[1] The brief, persuasive letter which Maitland wrote to Smuts encouraging him to think of the distinguished career that would lie before him as an academic lawyer, survives. [2] Mr. Graham, *African*, 837a.

attention', and where two or three members had a habit of engrossing its attention for their own business.¹ The majority in the Cabinet were not convinced of the need to act generously and at once in South Africa. It was Campbell-Bannerman who persuaded them to do so. Both Lloyd George and Lord Carrington wrote to the Prime Minister shortly after the decisive meeting, the one congratulating him on a magnificent piece of work in having 'saved the Government from inevitable disaster' and the other on 'having so magnificently saved the South African situation'.²

There followed from the Cabinet decision the abrogation of the Lyttelton constitution on February 13th and the announcement in the King's Speech opening the new Parliament on February 19, 1906, of the grant of self-government to the Transvaal and the Orange River Colony as soon as possible. Together they meant, as we have seen, that some four years after the defeat of the Boers and the overthrow of their indigenous administrations, the two former republics passed at one stroke from a status of complete subordination to a status, not of nominal but of effective self-government for their European inhabitants and of continuing subordination for their non-European peoples under new masters or, to be precise, old masters once more restored to authority. This was the outcome of a political decision. It may well have been insufficiently considered; it was certainly not unconsidered. And still less, be it repeated, was it the leap-in-the-dark it is sometimes represented to be. It was on one view a calculated risk and on another it was, as Campbell-Bannerman's biographer wrote, 'an act of faith'.³ It was the faith that was decisive.

Liberal faith in a generous settlement, applying the Durham

¹ R. B. Haldane, *An Autobiography* (London, Hodder & Stoughton, 1929), pp. 216–17. In Haldane's view neither Campbell-Bannerman nor Asquith after him sufficiently controlled Cabinet discussions. Morley, on the other hand, attributed to Campbell-Bannerman, 'as head of a Cabinet', a whole catalogue of virtues which seemingly escaped the notice of Haldane altogether. He was, in Morley's view, 'cool, acute, straight, candid, attentive to affairs, considerate'. *Recollections*, Vol. II, p. 143.

² J. A. Spender, *Campbell-Bannerman*, Vol. II, p. 238.

³ *Ibid.*, pp. 237–8.

THE MAGNANIMOUS GESTURE

panacea of responsible self-government to the former Boer republics, was not newly found but most notably in the person of the Prime Minister[1] had been long entertained. During the war he had recorded his belief that conditions in South Africa were very similar to those in British North America when Lord Durham reported on them. And Lord Durham in making his recommendations did not, so Campbell-Bannerman noted[2] in criticism of Chamberlain's ideas for a post-war South African settlement, propose to deprive French-Canadians of their language or their educational system, 'to swamp them with new settlers and to break their spirit by a course of Crown Colony Government. If he had we should have lost Canada. Nor did he take the emotions of the loyalists as the test of statesmanship.' On the contrary Lord Durham recommended responsible self-government with generous safeguards for French-speaking Canada and the result was that, to quote Campbell-Bannerman's words again, 'Canada remains as the greatest triumph of British statesmanship, of broad and liberal views and nobly instructed imagination'. It was this Canadian precedent that guided Campbell-Bannerman's thoughts on South Africa. From the outset of the war, as we have seen, he had accepted annexation as its inevitable outcome and throughout its course he testified publicly to his conviction that the essential Liberal contribution to the post-war settlement should be the grant of free and responsible government with no intermediary stage and as soon as conditions allowed. For this he had received the patronizing contempt of *The Times*. 'But Sir Henry Campbell-Bannerman',

[1] The opinions of the Liberal Imperialists, Rosebery, Haldane, Asquith and Grey on the essentials of the post-war settlement, were very different from those of Campbell-Bannerman. In May 1901, for example, Grey wrote to Milner of the need for 'the establishment of direct Imperial Administration for a time, with a view to eventual representative Colonial Government when the country has filled up and settled down'. C. Headlam, *The Milner Papers* (London, Cassell, 1933), Vol. II, p. 262. See Milner's correspondence with Haldane, *ibid.*, pp. 263–6.

[2] Add. MS. 41243A, f. 62. The quotations which follow are reproduced from notes made by Campbell-Bannerman for a speech, *ibid.*, ff. 56–80.

observed its editorial on October 19, 1900, 'in his efforts to be all things to all men, has failed to inspire confidence in anybody. After sitting on the fence as long as he could, he has climbed down, according to his habit, on the wrong side. He has committed himself at the last moment to the denunciation of any period of Crown Colony Government in the annexed states....'[1] *The Times*, on this as on other occasions, underestimated Campbell-Bannerman's foresight and a faith which in 1906 found a literal expression rare in politics.

The conviction that the immediate restoration of self-government was the right course to adopt, no doubt was the more easily confirmed in office with the thought that a transfer of authority to Pretoria would also mean the transfer there of responsibility for some delicate post-electoral issues as well as many administrative problems. Mr Churchill, indeed, felt impelled to warn his colleagues, 'We must not endeavour by the gift of Responsible Government to rid ourselves of our South African responsibilities. It would be very pleasant to throw the reins on the horse's neck, and very easy.'[2] Yet while the desire of politicians and civil servants to rid themselves of troublesome questions in far away places has more to do with Liberal imperial policies than many imperial historians care to allow, in this instance there was at root behind the decision of February 1906, long-standing conviction and the feeling that in respect of timing the moment for a gesture was right—as indeed it was, superbly right. 'They gave us back in everything but name—our country', said General Smuts. 'Has such a miracle of trust and magnanimity ever happened before?'

Even so well-timed a gesture could not obliterate all the memories of war. Grass may grow quickly over a battlefield but it grows slowly over burnt homesteads and civilian concentration camps—as any traveller in the Transvaal or the Orange Free State soon learns, it has not grown over them to this day. Nor did responsible government within the Empire compensate in all, or

[1] See also Spender, *Campbell-Bannerman*, Vol. II, p. 233.
[2] January 30, 1906. *African*, 817,

The Magnanimous Gesture

even most, Afrikaner minds for loss of republican independence, but at least it opened the way, as no other action conceivable in the circumstances could have done, for reconciliation. Within twelve years of the Raid which gave him his one enduring title to immortality, Dr Jameson, as Prime Minister of Cape Colony, is said to have acquired the habit of saying of General Louis Botha, first Prime Minister of the self-governing Transvaal (and from 1910 of the Union of South Africa), 'Botha is always right' —so much so that when someone told him that Botha had recommended his execution after the Raid, Jameson merely remarked, 'Botha is always right'. Even if the story be apocryphal the change in temper it implies unquestionably was real. On the death of Campbell-Bannerman in 1908 Botha wrote to Asquith saying that, 'in securing self-government for the new Colonies, he [Campbell-Bannerman] not only raised an imperishable monument to himself, but through the policy of trust he inspired the people of South Africa with a new feeling of hopefulness and co-operation. In making it possible for the two races to live and work together harmoniously he had laid the foundation of a united South Africa.'[1] By the two races, he meant the two white races: by a united South Africa, he meant a united white South Africa.

Though it seemed by no means so important in 1906 as it does today, it was the case that the white inhabitants formed no very large proportion of the population of the four colonies that were to comprise the Union of South Africa. The total, according to the census taken in 1904,[2] was nearly five and a quarter million. Of this number rather less than one and a quarter million were of European and rather more than four million of non-European descent. The Europeans who were the ruling race were divided then, as now, between Briton and Boer, or to be more exact between English-speaking or Dutch- or Afrikaans-speaking communities—Dutch being an official language of the Union till 1925 when it was replaced by the vernacular or Taal, which

[1] Spender, *Campbell-Bannerman*, Vol. II, pp. 395-6.
[2] See *State of the Union Year-Book for the Union of South Africa*, 1957, chapter 6.

is Afrikaans—in the proportion of about 45 to 55 per cent. But while the British were thus inferior in numbers they might be, and to some extent were, reinforced by new immigrants from the British Isles[1] and they had too, as the Boers never tired of saying, and rightly, another home and another country. Even when the imperial factor was of set policy excluded from the affairs of southern Africa it remained in being, capable of exercising a decisive influence on the course of events there. This was psychologically, as well as politically, important for Britons and Boers alike. The balance of numbers did not seem either to be of final significance for it was uncritically assumed that imperial weightage would come down invariably on the side of the English in South Africa.

Below the two European ruling groups, emerging from internecine struggle, were the subject peoples, comprising the vast majority of the inhabitants of the four South African colonies and themselves divided into three groups, the African Bantu, the Coloured, whom I once heard a Ceylonese diplomat describe all too romantically as the product of European gallantry and native indiscretion, and the Asiatics—Indian coolies working in the plantations of Natal and, for an interlude long enough to stir the conscience of English radicals and the fears of the English working man of cheap imported labour, Chinese mine-workers in the gold-fields on the Rand. In 1904 there were some half-million Coloured and little more than a hundred thousand Asiatics, though the slights and hardships from which they suffered sufficed to impel a young London-trained Indian lawyer, Mahatma Gandhi, to fashion in satyagraha a weapon of resistance so revolutionary in conception that Romain Rolland deemed the slight attention given to it in Europe to be 'une preuve de l'incroyable étroitesse d'horizon de nos hommes politiques, de nos historiens, de nos penseurs et de nos hommes de foi. . . .'[2]

---

[1] See N. H. Carrier and J. R. Jeffery, *External Migration 1815–1950* (London, H.M.S.O., 1953).

[2] Romain Rolland, *Mahatma Gandhi* (Paris, Librairie Stock, 1924), p. 17.

The Magnanimous Gesture

In the subject, as distinct from the nearly evenly divided ruling groups, there existed a possible foundation of unity in the great and growing Bantu majority. But it was, inevitably, in the circumstances of the time, not the seeming unity of the lower caste but the evident division in the ruling European group that occupied the first attention of the Liberal administration. In this their sense of perspective was surely just. The Europeans alone could assume at that time responsibility for self-government. Yet if power is to be transferred to a multi-racial society it is of critical importance to decide not only to whom it should be transferred in the first instance but also with what degree of finality it should be vested in their hands. The second was a matter which, it may be seen in retrospect, the Liberal Government weighed but weighed insufficiently.

For some sixty years British statesmen had conceived of a Federation in South Africa. Some had been content to abide for opportunity; others, including men so diverse in temper and outlook as the fourth Earl of Carnarvon, familiarly known to Disraeli as 'Twitters', Joseph Chamberlain, the only man in British history who refused the Exchequer to take the Colonial Office and one who impressed a German Chancellor,[1] but not all British historians, as being 'very scrupulous', and Alfred Milner, one of the finest products of Balliol scholarship in its greatest age, who spoke of the impossibility of conciliating the Boers with their 'panoplied hatred, insensate ambitions, invincible ignorance'[2] and who could never forgive the last, had tried to hasten it by forceful negotiation or by force itself. In the end something more than federation came, not through imposition of a central authority from without and above, but through the political withdrawal of the external imperial factor. Campbell-Bannerman's policy of 1906–7 thus did not bring about the unification of South Africa, but made it possible. His Government had the wisdom to recognize that this was something

---

[1] von Bülow in 1899. *Die Grosse Politik der Europäischen Kabinette 1871–1914*, Vol. XV, p. 423.

[2] May 25, 1901. *Milner Papers*, Vol. II, p. 254.

that, after the South African war, could be effected, if at all, only from within. The 'Imperial factor' therefore had to be, and was, firmly excluded. That was a condition of Afrikaner support for Union.

Before Union was accomplished there was a twofold change in the higher direction of imperial policy. Campbell-Bannerman resigned on April 6th and died on April 22, 1908. Asquith, who succeeded him, brought greater intellectual power but less intuitive understanding to South African affairs. His speeches and his actions suggest that he was content to follow where Campbell-Bannerman had led. Asquith dispensed, however, and unceremoniously, with Lord Elgin's services at the Colonial Office; that unfortunate peer's impending dismissal being first made known by *The Daily Chronicle*, he himself being later the recipient of a letter from the new Prime Minister containing allusion to the need for advancing younger men but making no acknowledgement of Elgin's services and by way of adding insult to injury concluding with the query: 'What about a Marquessate?'[1] In Mr Winston Churchill's view there was one man with outstanding qualifications for the vacant post—and that was Mr Winston Churchill. He submitted his claims to Asquith: 'I *know* the Colonial Office', he wrote. 'It is a post of immense, but largely disconnected detail; and I have special experiences of several kinds which helps. During the last two years practically all the constructive action and all the Parliamentary exposition has been mine.' 'The Government', he concluded, 'has much to gain from a spirited yet not improvident administration of an Imperial Department.'[2] Asquith remained seemingly unattracted by the prospect. He may indeed have thought a provident but not dispirited administration of imperial

[1] Sir Almeric Fitzroy, *Memoirs* (London, Hutchinson, n.d.) 2 vols., Vol. I, p. 348. Asquith and Elgin had been contemporaries at Balliol which made the manner of the dismissal the more surprising. There is a letter from Elgin to Asquith dated April 13, 1908, in the Asquith Papers at the Bodleian Library expressing regret if in an earlier letter he (Elgin) 'did not sufficiently recognize your appreciation of my work. . . .'

[2] Churchill to Asquith, March 14, 1908. Asquith Papers, Dep. 11.

The Magnanimous Gesture

affairs more in accord with the outlook of the rank and file of the party than the variant Mr Churchill suggested. In any event, Lord Crewe, pliable and persuasive, became Colonial Secretary and Mr Churchill went to the Board of Trade. Under the new dispensation the South African policy to which the Liberal Government was committed was prudently pursued but something of the conviction and dramatic force of its earlier presentation had departed.

In accordance with Canadian and Australian precedents, the constitution of the Union of South Africa was fashioned by representatives of the self-governing colonies concerned, Cape Colony, Natal, the Transvaal and the Orange River Colony in debate and after much hard bargaining first at Durban and then at Bloemfontein. How it was made has been told in a magisterial study by Professor L. M. Thompson of the University of Cape Town.[1] From the Commonwealth viewpoint the most important thing was that it was in Lord Selborne's phrase 'home-made'.[2] That meant that the preconceptions and preoccupations of those who made it, and not of the Imperial Government, determined its character. Yet the responsibility of the Imperial Government remained. They had long been the principal protagonists of a united South Africa, now by their magnanimity they had opened the way to Union and ultimately, by legislative enactment, the Imperial Parliament had to sanction its constitution. The first step, indeed, predicated the second. They took it also—and magnanimously—with the enactment of the South Africa Act of 1909 which embodied the constitution of the Union of South Africa.

The Price

In all human affairs magnanimous gestures customarily exact a price—otherwise indeed they might be more usual occurrences

[1] L. M. Thompson, *The Unification of South Africa 1902–1910* (Oxford at the Clarendon Press, 1960).

[2] Cf. Lord Crewe's reference, House of Lords Debates, 1909, Vol. II, col. 755.

—but it is not necessarily the man or nation that makes the gesture that pays the price. Did the British Government and people pay the price of their magnanimous gestures in South Africa? Or did they make the gestures and not have to pay the price? May it be reasonably urged that it was not Englishmen, but English-speaking South Africans (at least outside the ranks of the wealthy mine-owning magnates), who paid some part of that price? May it not be much more forcibly urged that the Bantu or non-European generally, who had no voice in the making of Union, has paid the major part of it? The gesture of 1906, the Union of 1910, does not excite their warm regard. 'In 1960', said Mr Duma Nokwe, Secretary of the African National Congress, 'it will be exactly fifty years since Britain sold out the rights of Africans with the Act of Union.'[1]

When the South Africa Act had passed through Parliament Botha wrote to Asquith saying that it was due 'to the far seeing policy of your party, carried out bravely in most difficult circumstances, that all has gone so well in South Africa and that its position as an integral part of the British Empire has become assured. There are many today who claim a larger or smaller share of the credit in connection with the realization of Union in South Africa but this one thing is certain, that only the Liberal policy of your Government has made that Union possible.'[2] Asquith marking the last phrase in the margin of the letter communicated the substance of it, together with a tribute somewhat more guarded in tone if even more impressive in origin from J. H. Hofmeyr to his Sovereign.[3] And to Botha he replied with unconcealed satisfaction: 'There is nothing in our conduct of affairs during the last four years on which we look back with so much satisfaction as the full and free grant of self-government to the Transvaal and the Orange River Colony, which has rendered possible that which, at our advent to power, seemed an unrealizable dream—the Union of South

[1] *The Observer*, December 13, 1959.
[2] Asquith Papers, Dep. 12. Botha to Asquith, August 23, 1909.
[3] *Ibid.*, letter dated August 26, 1909.

Africa.'[1] Yet today, and despite the mutual self-congratulation of Boer and British Prime Ministers, the question is hardly to be evaded, would it have been better in view of the price to be exacted of others had the dream never been realized?

[1] Asquith Papers, and also reprinted in Spender and Asquith, *op. cit.*, Vol. 1, p. 267.

2

THE PRICE FOR ENGLISH-SPEAKING SOUTH AFRICANS

> The Boers have, like all of us, some good qualities and a good many bad ones, and among their qualities which Hon. Members may class as good or bad according to their fancy, they are stubborn, they are self-sufficient, they are unimpressionable, they are shrewd and they are brave....
>
> SIR HENRY CAMPBELL-BANNERMAN
> House of Commons, October 17, 1899

Today relations between the two European peoples in South Africa are thought to be of quite secondary importance everywhere except in South Africa itself. Fifty years ago it was not so. It was relations between Dutch and British that were almost universally regarded as of paramount importance and they were spoken of inaccurately but, in the circumstances, not inappropriately, in terms of race. They were deemed to constitute 'the racial issue', relations between European and African being terminologically relegated to the 'Native Question'. In so far as imperial statesmen had entertained the idea of a self-governing federal or unitary state in southern Africa comprising the British territories of Cape Colony and Natal and the two trekker republics, they had to think of the future relations between the ruling peoples, between Dutch and English, and having done so to consider the alternatives of a state united with Britain, as were the Pacific dominions and Canada, by the ties of kinship on the part at least of the majority of that ruling European population or alternatively of Anglo-Dutch reconciliation on the basis of a

The Price for English-Speaking South Africans

common South African and a common imperial loyalty. The first, in view of Boer numerical preponderance, could be secured only by large-scale British immigration. That was the course Lord Milner favoured. 'Absolutely everything', he wrote in a memorandum dated November 8, 1901, 'depends upon starting the new self-governing Confederation with a British-minded majority. We must wait for Federation and self-government until that majority is assured.'[1] In this respect Milner followed Lord Durham who had conceived British preponderance in North America to be essential for keeping French-Canadians abreast of the great nineteenth-century march of progress. But time and circumstances were different. The nineteenth century was over, its simple faith in progress overcast, while the events of the last decade had left the reputation of British political leadership at the Cape and still more in the Transvaal sadly tarnished. Even to the most perfervid of patriots, the mine-owners of the Rand—those 'fine old English Gentlemen' as Michael Davitt ironically described them before listing their names—Beit, Wernher, Eckstein, Rouilot, Barnato, Adler, Lowe, Wolff, Goldmann, Neumann and Goertz[2]—unconvincing as martyrs, inept as revolutionaries, seemed out of place as the standard-bearers of British enlightenment, while to their more radical fellow-countrymen eagerly absorbing the Hobsonian dialectic simple-minded Boer farmers, however retrograde in their political and social outlook, had at least as much to commend

[1] *Milner Papers* (London, Cassell, 1931–3), Vol. II, pp. 279–80. Characteristically he worked out statistically how this might be achieved. At the end of the war there would be a white population of 940,000 composed of 496,000 Dutch, 368,000 British and 76,000 other Whites. With favourable British immigration policies and the industrial expansion of the Transvaal the scales might be turned so that out of a population of 1,270,000 there could be 615,000 British, 544,000 Dutch and 111,000 other Whites. On the basis of one member to every 10,000 Whites these figures would give 64 British to 58 Dutch Members in a Federal Assembly. The Afrikaners never forgot Milner's calculations when, later, questions of British immigration were raised.

[2] House of Commons Debates, Vol. LXXVII, October 17, 1899, col. 125.

them as plutocrats who had dragged their fellow-countrymen into an unnecessary and unjustifiable imperialist adventure in order to swell the profits from their own investments.[1] Besides there was the awkward fact that there were more Boers than Britons in southern Africa. Milner might urge that this unsatisfactory position should be remedied by bringing in Britons to redress the balance and that till that was done final authority should continue to rest in London. But the day of enforced plantations was also over and what if, as soon became apparent, enough Britons were not prepared of their own free will to go? Did not that expose the policy as impracticable even if it were not also misconceived? Yet if this were so, what then remained for the Unionists other than the continued assertion of imperial power? Chamberlain in the eve of war speech in which he had complained so bitterly of President Kruger's procrastinating replies and of his dribbling out of reforms 'like water from a squeezed sponge' had promised that if the Unionist Government were compelled to take 'this matter in hand we will not let it go until we have secured conditions which shall once for all establish which is the paramount power in South Africa. . . .'[2] It was established, but not once for all. That was the Unionist dilemma.

The Liberals did not think in terms of perpetual British paramountcy. They entertained more sanguine opinions of human nature, and particularly of Boer human nature. 'Paramountcy?

[1] On the eve of the war John Morley warned that 'such a war of the strongest government in the world against this weak little Republic . . . may give greater buoyancy to the South African stock and share market . . . may send the price of Mr Rhodes's Chartereds up to a point beyond the dream of avarice . . . but even then it will be wrong'. *The Times*, September 22, 1899. In the House of Commons on October 17, 1899, Labouchere, echoing Morley's thoughts, complained 'there has been a great deal too much of the Stock Exchange element in the matter', and stated that the reputedly overtaxed mine-owners were making fortunes 'beyond the dreams of avarice' and that the war was one of 'a medium-sized English town against the greatest and mightiest Empire'. House of Commons Debates, Vol. LXXVII, coll. 107-9.

[2] *The Times*, August 28, 1899.

The Price for English-Speaking South Africans

No. ... Do not say to one race, You are to be at the top and the other shall be at the bottom. No. Let there be fusion not paramountcy.' Such were the terms of Morley's rejoinder to Chamberlain in a speech to his constituents at Arbroath in September 1899.[1] And Morley recoiled from the very thought of a war to secure paramountcy by the crushing of a little state. It was something not to be considered, for it would bring deep national dishonour, and—a characteristically British reflection—it would set such an example 'to the armed camps and scheming Chanceries of continental Europe' as would cast a shadow upon the closing years of the Queen's reign. 'Yes, Empire, they say, Empire. Yes, but we do not want a pirate Empire.' But once the war had begun, and still more when the Empire, whether 'pirate' or not,[2] was about to absorb the spoils, condemnation hardly sufficed as a policy. The Liberals had now to think in terms of the future of a South Africa in which British power would be paramount. What was to be their attitude in these changed circumstances? It was no longer a question of whether or not to go to war, but on what terms to make peace with the Boers. This was the question that Campbell-Bannerman attempted to answer without abandoning what he conceived to be essential Liberal principles. While he roundly condemned the policy of subjugation and the demand for unconditional surrender, he did not shirk a public answer to the question of what should be the future relation of the British to the Boers in South Africa. 'What', he asked in 1902,[3] 'is the desire of all of us for the future of South Africa? Surely it is not only that there should be peace and freedom from the danger of internal hostilities throughout that vast future Dominion of the Crown: not only that equal rights should be established. ...

[1] *The Times*, September 6, 1899. Both this and the extracts from the two preceding speeches are quoted in S. Maccoby, *English Radicalism 1886–1914* (London, Allen & Unwin, 1953), chapter XVI.

[2] John Dillon spoke, as might be expected, in stronger terms of an 'atrocious war of plunder, piracy and robbery'. House of Commons Debates, October 23, 1899, col. 527.

[3] Spender, *Campbell-Bannerman*, Vol. II, p. 21.

We want something more than that: we want amity and close brotherhood between the races: and this golden age can only be reached if the settlement is one between brave and friendly and mutually respectful foes, and not a mere surly and sulky submission to the conqueror.'

The peace, negotiated by Unionists and received by the Liberals with a lack of criticism that betokened approval of, rather than mere acquiescence in the terms of a generous treaty, in effect fulfilled the first part of the prescribed conditions: it remained for the Liberal Government to complete the settlement. Their policy was founded on trust; trust on the part of Britain that the Boers, generously treated, would be loyal to the imperial connexion; trust on the part of the Boers that the imperial factor would be withdrawn from South Africa; trust on the part of the English-speaking South Africans that the Boers would not use the superior voting power of greater numbers against them. Britain was well placed to protect her interests should need arise but if the confidence of the Boers in the final withdrawal of the imperial factor proved well-founded and that of the English-speaking South Africans in respect of voting power ill-founded, then English-speaking South Africans might be called upon to pay no small part of the price of imperial magnanimity. It was a possibility entertained with gloomy foreboding by Unionist opponents of Liberal policy and discounted neither by the Government nor still less their official advisers.

'The worst and most dangerous of all the disservices which that party [the Liberal] has rendered to our country', complained Milner at Johannesburg in 1902,[1] 'is that by their eternal clamour they keep the thoughts of their countrymen with regard to South Africa in one particular rut. They will never convert them to pro-Boerism, but they do make the figure of the Boer loom too large in the British imagination.... "Will this form of settlement conciliate the Boer or will that form of settlement conciliate him better? Such and such a policy may be all very well but will it annoy the Boers?" Morning, noon, and night

[1] *Milner Papers*, Vol. II, pp. 320–1.

it is Boers, Boers, Boers. But what of all the rest of South African humanity? ... as a nation we really cannot indulge in this high degree of altruism at the expense of our friends.' This, it need hardly be said, was overstatement. It was the exploits of Boer commandos viewed in romantic retrospect coupled with the sense that restitution was due to a small, gallant and defeated enemy that chiefly predisposed British people towards a final and generous settlement with the Boers. There was also a recoil from some of 'our friends', including Dr Jameson as well as the mine-owners, of which the Boers were no doubt the beneficiaries. But 'Liberal clamour' during the war unquestionably played a significant contributory part. Yet distrust of the Boer remained pronounced. In the spring of 1906 and after his return from London Smuts wrote to Chief Justice de Villiers, who was later to preside over the National Convention at Durban, about the 'strong apprehensions as to our future line of policy' that must be lurking in the minds of members of the West Ridgeway Committee (which had been appointed by the Liberal Cabinet to prepare for responsible self-government in the Transvaal) and he recalled: 'The fear of us I found quite general in England—even in the most liberal quarters.'[1] He was right. It was in particular something very present to the minds of the Government's official advisers, and some at least of the misgivings they entertained were neither wholly without foundation nor without continuing relevance today.

How would the British portion of the population fare under a dominant Boer party in the Transvaal, enquired Mr Graham, the Assistant Under-Secretary at the Colonial Office, in December 1905. 'It is not safe to prophesy unless you know', he wrote in answer to his own question, with a fine opening concession to the tradition of civil service caution before proceeding more boldly, 'but I venture to predict that if the grant of responsible government ... resulted in the formation of a dominant Boer party, the British population outside the mining magnates and

[1] E. A. Walker, *Lord de Villiers and His Times* (London, Constable, 1925), pp. 418–19.

speculators, who are able to take care of themselves, would fare badly while the hope that the Boers could become reconciled to British rule might be for ever abandoned.' The interest of the Boer farmer would be cared for but 'would he be taught the gospel of reconciliation? I very much doubt it. In the Cape Colony the greatest enemies we have had to encounter are the "Predicant" of the Dutch Reformed Church and the Schoolmaster.'[1] From South Africa Lord Selborne in a despatch to Lord Elgin sought for his part to assess the future line of Boer policy. He underlined the strength of the Boer tradition of leadership. 'Every Boer who is not bed-ridden will always vote at an election, and he will always vote without fail for the man for whom his leaders tell him to vote.' As a result, in the High Commissioner's opinion, the whole Boer people from the Cape to the Zambesi would be directed by a small body of educated men who 'with the exception of the fighting generals Botha, De la Rey, and de Wet, are not farmers, but professional men living in towns, and educated in Europe'.[2] The ideal they entertained, which governed all their thoughts and actions, was to form 'a United Republic of South Africa, to which British Colonials will be gladly admitted but only on condition it is a Republic with its own flag and that the predominant influence is not British but Boer'. And some months later he foretold that the giving of a majority to the Boers four years after the war 'would result in the separation from the British Empire of the Transvaal and eventually of South Africa'.[3]

Neither Mr Graham nor Lord Selborne were well disposed to Boer claims or Liberal gestures—and at one point indeed Lord Selborne incurred rebuke from his home Government for his evident lack of support for some aspects of its policy—but in 1961 one cannot fail to be impressed by the extent to which the forecasts of both men have been fulfilled. Smuts in his memorandum discounted party divisions on 'racial' lines[4] but on the long

[1] *African*, 796C.
[2] Selborne to Elgin, December 14, 1905. *African*, 812.
[3] *Ibid.*, May 12, 1906, C.O. 291/99.   [4] See above, p. 27.

THE PRICE FOR ENGLISH-SPEAKING SOUTH AFRICANS

view and despite all the endeavours of Botha and of Smuts himself party divisions on near 'racial' lines have emerged. Within Afrikanerdom the prestige of the leaders remains exceptional;[1] the influence of the predikants and schoolmasters are but little abated. The goal of an Afrikaner republic has been pursued by succeeding generations and is now attained. Yet though the prognostications of Assistant Under-Secretary and High Commissioner proved in the main well-founded that is not tantamount to saying that the withholding of self-government would have produced, even from an exclusively British standpoint, more beneficial results. It does, however, underline the vulnerability of the position of the English-speaking community in South Africa under representative institutions.

From the outset it was apparent that self-government first in the Transvaal and later in South Africa with a restricted European franchise meant that political power would rest with the larger European community. Certainly it is true that the Afrikaners, unfamiliar as they were in the two defeated republics with the processes of representative government, did not wholly understand at first the power which electoral arithmetic was to give them. They felt, as General Hertzog was apt to complain, as step-children in their own home.[2] Their attitude in consequence was defensive; but even so, the Boer leaders in the Transvaal did not overlook the fact that given party division on cultural lines, then under representative government, only large-scale English immigration could prevent the defeated Boers from coming back into their own again. It was because this was so that there was much debate, both in the Transvaal and in London, on voting rights and delimitation of constituencies once self-government was restored.

The crucial question in this debate, on the answer to which

[1] On this point see G. M. Carter, *The Politics of Inequality. South Africa since 1948* (New York, F. A. Praeger, 1958), Section IV especially.

[2] Cf. C. M. van den Heever, *General J. B. M. Hertzog* (Johannesburg, 1946), p. 137.

turned the future balance of electoral power in the Transvaal, was whether constituencies should be delimited on an adult male, or on a general, population basis, the former being likely to yield a non-Boer majority because of the large number[1] of unmarried British miners on the Rand and the latter certain to give a Boer one. Two men, Smuts and Churchill, their years of greatest fame and warm-hearted collaboration before them, contributed their views on this vexing issue. On Smuts's side it was one of the points to which he gave very considerable attention in his memorandum.[2] 'The principle of one-vote-one-value', he argued in a passage marked blue in the margin in Asquith's copy,[3] 'is unsound, and a misnomer, as it really gives a higher value to a vote on the Rand than in the rest of the Transvaal, and undemocratic, as it assumes that the State consists only of qualified male adults, and neglects not only the unqualified, but also the women and children who constitute from many points of view the most important part of the population and an asset infinitely more important than all the gold and diamond mines in the country.' If such a principle were adopted, responsible government, he continued in a passage underlined this time in red in Asquith's copy, 'will simply substitute the mine-owners for the Colonial Office in the government of the Transvaal and the Boers would rather have an indefinite period of Crown Colony administration than see the Transvaal permanently put under the government of the financial magnates'. Smuts stood accordingly, though not necessarily for precisely these reasons, for delimitation on a population basis and 'for nothing less'. 'This is', reported the High Commissioner,[4] 'a very natural position for the Boers to take up. What they want is the certainty of such a majority as will secure to them the permanent Government of the country.' Such a majority could be secured either, as Smuts advocated, by a constituency delimitation which would give due weight to the

[1] Estimated at about 80 per cent of the total number.
[2] See above, p. 27.   [3] Asquith Papers, Dep. 19.
[4] Selborne to Elgin, March 12, 1906, C.O. 291/97.

The Price for English-Speaking South Africans

numerical preponderance of the Boers in the rural districts or even by extending the vote to women. The Progressives and the Responsible Government Association, on the other hand, favoured delimitation on the basis of one vote, one value, the vote being restricted to adult males; and they would have in addition preferred a property qualification, such as had been contemplated in the Lyttelton constitution, to remain. The *raison d'être* of the demand for one vote one value, noted a Colonial Office official, 'is to create a British majority'.[1] That indeed was why the Parliamentary Under-Secretary of State approved it so warmly. It was vital to future imperial interests in South Africa, noted Mr Churchill, to build up a powerful and well-organized British, or at the least non-Dutch party, and here was a well-chosen means for doing so. 'One vote one value, single member districts and automatic redistribution', he pointed out, 'are devices unassailable on democratic grounds. ... It is not often that democratic principles are helpful in imperial administration. When they are they should be cherished.'[2] The Committee under the chairmanship of Sir Joseph West Ridgeway sent out to determine this among other issues in part cherished them, but made their conclusion the more acceptable to the Boers by accompanying recommendations to abolish all property qualification and to transfer two seats from the Rand to rural districts.[3] There followed, with English-speaking support and to their own professed surprise, the victory of the Het Volk in the first Transvaal election with Botha taking office as first Prime Minister in March 1907. Boer political predominance in the Transvaal was restored and it foreshadowed their predominance in a united South Africa in which the Transvaal by reason of its wealth, its population and its leadership was destined to hold the key.

A variety of other devices or safeguards more or less consistent with the larger aim of winning Afrikaner loyalties by trusting Afrikaners were contemplated in London for the numerically

[1] *Ibid.* Minute dated March 13. [2] *African*, 804, minute January 2, 1906.
[3] See C.O. 291/112 for text of Committee's Report.

weaker, but politically and economically stronger, European community in the Transvaal. Such discussions are apt to pursue familiar and unprofitable courses and this occasion proved no exception. Some concerned themselves with possible protection of settlers' rights; others, including Mr Churchill and Lord Selborne, went Second Chambering and some of those who had been forward in urging the merits of self-government, contemplated ways in which some of its substance might be whittled away so long as, to quote Mr Churchill, 'race hatred' was 'still red hot from war'. But among the most carefully considered means of reinsuring the future position of the still dominant European minority and one touching an issue of fundamental cultural importance was the assertion in the constitution of an exclusive language.

In 1906 there were thought to be three languages, any one of which might become firmly established as the dominant language in South Africa—English, Afrikaans and Dutch. The High Commissioner, noting that the Taal (Afrikaans) and English were the common languages of the people from the Cape to the Zambezi and that 'the Boers have the same affection for the Taal as the Welsh have for Welsh', unlike Lord Milner in his later phase, favoured full freedom for the use of the Taal at the sole discretion of the new Legislature in the Transvaal. This was in accord with the existing practice in the Courts. But why did Lord Selborne favour such freedom? Because the Taal, unlike Welsh, was not a written language and had 'no literature'. 'Consequently, although in my opinion the Taal will be a language of affection and patriotism in South Africa for centuries to come, from the political point of view there is no reason for any jealousy between English and the Taal.' But High Dutch was another matter. Lord Selborne considered anxiously whether the leaders of the Boer Afrikander Party, of the Bond and Het Volk and the Predikants might not seek to win preeminence for High Dutch because, returning once again to an oft-repeated theme, 'these gentlemen do not acquiesce in the permanent inclusion of South Africa within the British Empire'

The Price for English-Speaking South Africans

but rather 'desire to form a separate United States of South Africa'.[1] The High Commissioner's misgivings were gravely weighed in the Colonial Office and the Secretary of State gave no recorded sign of attending, as closely as historians are likely to do, to a much-erased minute, which has indeed all the appearance of a first draft for the peroration of a speech, signed W. S. C. In it the Parliamentary Under-Secretary, noting that 'in all these petty burning questions wisdom indicates the line of least resistance', stated unequivocally, 'I am for complete bilingual equality', and went on to express little fear of High Dutch, a language not rooted in the soil, ousting English, 'the dominant literary and commercial medium of speech, even if that were intrinsically a less powerful language, instead of being the most flexible, forceful, widespread and magnificent of modern tongues'.[2]

The line of least resistance in respect of language was, in fact, followed in the Transvaal and later in South Africa. General Hertzog, who was the great champion not merely of the principle of equality but of effective equality, told the National Convention in Durban that the Dutch people of South Africa would never accept a settlement which left the absolute equality of their language with English in doubt. Section 137 of the South Africa Act embodied the principle of equality, though leaving open how it should be applied. It was one of the provisions of the Act which was entrenched. Originally its purpose was defensive from the Afrikaner point of view. But with the passage of time a remarkable reversal in attitude took place. Less and less was it the Afrikaners and more and more was it the English-speaking South Africans who underlined the rights assured to them in Section 137 of the South Africa Act. With

[1] Selborne to Elgin, April 23, 1906, C.O. 291/98.

[2] *Ibid.*, minute May 31, 1906. Churchill did not join the Cabinet till April 1908. Haldane, who felt in retrospect that he himself ought to have taken a more active part in Cabinet business, found Churchill 'as long-winded as he was persistent'. *Autobiography* (London, Hodder & Stoughton, 1929), p. 217. The Secretary of State may have entertained not dissimilar views about some of his minutes.

continuing failure to create one white South Africa the implications of electoral arithmetic in two were increasingly realized. In the draft republican constitution, first published in *Die Transvaler* on January 23, 1942, it was stated that 'Afrikaans, as the language of the original white inhabitants of the country, will be the first official language' and that English as a second or supplementary language would enjoy equal rights, freedom and privileges with the first official language, 'everywhere and whereever such treatment is judged by the State Authority to be in the best interests of the State and its inhabitants'. This represented not a final judgement but a trend of thinking among Afrikaner nationalists on the language question. In the republican constitution of South Africa, which came into force on May 31, 1961, equal language rights remained entrenched as in the South Africa Act of 1909. But none the less the linguistic position of the numerically weaker community was felt in some degree to have been imperilled since the accession of the Nationalist Government to power in 1948 and to that extent members of it have since then been shadowed by the thought that, if Campbell-Bannerman's act of faith does not prove justified in the long run, it is they who will pay the linguistic price.[1]

Language is the cherished symbol of cultural identity and the Imperial Government's attention to the language question was surely well placed. But neither their power nor the measure of their responsibility should be exaggerated in this or in other respects. By their actions in 1906–7 the Liberal Government opened the way to closer association between the South African colonies henceforward enjoying equality of status. They did not bear responsibility for the form of that closer association or for

[1] The draft republican constitution of 1942 was one factor accentuating their fears: another was the extending influence and activities of the Broederbond, a secret society which only those may join who are Afrikaans-speaking, of the Protestant faith and who accept South Africa as their only homeland. For fuller comment see Mansergh, *Survey of British Commonwealth Affairs 1939–52*, pp. 157–8, on the first, and Carter, *op. cit.*, pp. 251–6, on the second.

the degree of protection it afforded to the political or cultural interests of the two white communities. That was a matter for the Colonial Governments to decide in conference and it was their representatives who, in fact, decided that they would prefer union to federation. This was a decision of critical importance, carried through chiefly by pressure from the Transvaal.

The aim of the architects of Union was the fusing of the two European races and thereby, to quote General Smuts, 'the remaking of South Africa . . . on a higher plane of political and national life'. The unitary form of government, subject to whatever safeguards were agreed, was chosen partly because of a desire for economy in administration, but chiefly because it was thought the more likely to weld white South Africa 'into one compact nationality inspired by one common pervading spirit', and, be it added, applying one consistent and coherent native policy. It meant and, despite some superficial appearance to the contrary, was understood by the powerful Transvaal delegation to the Convention to mean, strong, centralized government with ultimate authority resting in the Union Parliament. It meant also, as federation would not have done, that if the experiment of fusion failed then the majority white community would be well placed to control the government of the country should it so desire. The Canadian precedent, which had ensured perhaps only too successfully the safeguarding of French-Canadian rights, was deemed inappropriate partly because of very different financial, trading and transport problems and still more because the European peoples were intermingled in South Africa as they were not in Canada. But it is also true that the counterbalancing advantages of a federal system were insufficiently weighed because of the deficiencies of the colonial government, and the indolence and ineptitude of the political leaders in Natal, the one province which had a clear interest on almost every political and cultural ground in federation rather than union. As a result the case for federation went almost by default. 'I could always in the last resort', wrote Patrick Duncan, 'ask opponents in Natal whether under unification 'they thought their affairs would be more inefficiently managed than they are now and none of them could truthfully say that their worst apprehension went as far as that.'¹ Union was in fact approved in Natal, alone of the four provinces, by popular referendum. More than anything else this illustrates the impressive degree of confidence that prevailed in the principle of one white South African nation at that time. But it was also an early reflection of the comparative indifference of English-speaking South Africans to politics. Even during the Convention many of them preferred their evening game of bridge to the hard thinking given to important points of constitutional drafting by the Transvaal delegation. The Union, in a fuller sense than need have been the case, was Transvaal-made with Cape amendments.

Though the imperial factor played no direct part in the shaping of the Union none the less English-speaking South Africans continued to repose their ultimate faith upon it. They could, so they thought, in consequence, afford to leave politics to the Afrikaners and attend to their financial and commercial enterprises. For the first thirty-eight years of the Union's life its Prime Ministers were all Boers and Boer Generals at that.² For the whole fifty-one years of the Union's existence they were all Afrikaners but, regrettably as it may now seem in retrospect, not all Generals. Of course, unless there were fusion of the two white races, Afrikaner political predominance was something to be anticipated. But virtual English-speaking exclusion from the higher ranges of politics was not. At first it did not seem to them to matter. The counsels of Botha and Smuts were so evidently enlightened that with the passing of passions 'red hot from war' they would surely prevail! Besides, and if they did not, was not the South Africa Act itself an act of the Imperial Parliament? Little did most English-speaking South Africans foresee that that Act was to prove a milestone in the decentralization of

¹ Quoted Thompson, *op. cit.*, p. 169.
² Professor D. W. Krüger's history of the Union from 1910 to 1948 was appropriately entitled *The Age of the Generals*.

imperial authority and the acceptance of a policy, always to be associated with the name of Generals Botha and Smuts, of decentralization to the limit in Commonwealth affairs.[1]

In 1931 the Imperial Parliament formally divested itself of its overriding legislative authority. It was in turn assumed by the Union Parliament and legally asserted in the Status of the Union Act, 1934. Time elapsed once again before either English-speaking South Africans, or still more Afrikaner Nationalists generally realized the full significance of the change and the extent of the power now vested in the Parliament and Government of the Union. So much indeed was evident from the speeches of many members made in the course of the protracted debate that took place in the House of Assembly in early September 1939 when by the narrow margin of thirteen votes the House rejected the motion of the Prime Minister, General Hertzog, for South Africa's neutrality and accepted the amendment to it proposed by the Deputy Prime Minister, General Smuts, for South Africa's participation in the war against Nazi Germany. And even more remarkable, despite the decision so dramatically reached by South Africa's elected representatives in Parliament assembled, Nationalists remained persuaded that while, as in 1914 so in 1939, South Africa might have a free constitution she did not have a free Government. This was the 'terrible condition of affairs' of which Mr Strijdom spoke in August 1940 and he maintained that there was only one way of getting rid of it and that was 'by doing away with this British connection and getting a free South African Republic. Then we could not be dragged into such a war as we have now been dragged into.... I say that our national pride and sense of

---

[1] At the Imperial Conference of 1911 General Botha said: 'It is the policy of decentralization which has made the British Empire.' (Cd. 5745, p. 42.) In his address to the Empire Parliamentary Association on November 25, 1943, General Smuts said: 'In the Commonwealth we follow to the limit the principle of decentralization.' Reprinted Mansergh, *Documents and Speeches on British Commonwealth Affairs 1931-52*, Vol. I, p. 572.

independence demands that we should break the British connection and establish a republic. . . . As long as the British flag flies in South Africa, as long as the English King is also our King, and as long as the Englishman in South Africa over and above having his Union citizenship also remains a British subject ... as long as we have the position that one section of the population stands planted with both feet on South African soil while the other section unfortunately gives its loyalty and love not to South Africa but to Great Britain . . . so long shall we fail to have unity here.' Nothing, it was apparent, from this catalogue of grievance and frustration would finally convince Afrikanerdom that South Africa was free until the republic was restored.

Before that final goal was reached experience brought a fuller understanding of the autonomy that South Africa had acquired within the Commonwealth and so prepared the way for the Nationalist Government's expressed desire for a continuing membership once that had been accepted in 1949, in respect of India, as consistent with full republican independence. 'But after South Africa became a conquered country and a colony of Britain's', Mr Strijdom, now Prime Minister of the Union, pointed out in 1957,[2] 'a very interesting development took place in the composition of the British Empire. Some of the Crown Colonies, as a result of legislation passed by the British Parliament, first developed into self-governing colonies; and later on some of them, as a result of an agreement with the British Government, countries such as Canada, Australia and South Africa developed into sovereign independent countries, bound together in what was formerly called the British Commonwealth and what is now called simply the Commonwealth.' He said well but the only notable thing about what he said was that he still thought it worth while saying in 1957.

But still independence within the Commonwealth but without the republic was not enough. The heart of Afrikanerdom did

[1] House of Assembly Debates, Vol. 40, coll. 324–5.
[2] *Ibid.*, February 1, 1957, Vol. 93, coll. 482–3.

The Price for English-Speaking South Africans

not warm to an advance in accord with the evolutionary processes of the British liberal tradition. There had been a conquest; it was not enough that it should be in practice quietly undone. It had to be reversed by outward and dramatic sign. The symbols so dear to Afrikanerdom had to be restored and recognized as the only symbols to be cherished by all true South Africans. The existence of this psychological need was clearly brought out by the Prime Minister, Mr Strijdom, in the debate on the National Flag from which a quotation has already been made. In it he thus interpreted the sequence of events in respect of that visible symbol of nationhood. 'The fact', he said,[1] 'that the Union Jack which flies in South Africa today is the flag of another independent country is, of course, due to the fact that South Africa is or was a conquered country and, as happens in all conquered countries, whether the conqueror be Britain or Germany or France, the flag of the conqueror flies in that conquered country.' In 1926–7 but for the strength of the feeling of 'the English-speaking people in this country in those days that they still formed part of the British nation and that for that reason Britain's national flag, i.e. the Union Jack, was also their flag', General Hertzog's Government would have given the Union 'one flag only, namely the national flag'. Instead there was compromise and the two flags. But with recognized and established independence there was no place for continuing compromise. 'A country's national flag, like its national anthem, is one of the strongest outward symbols of nationhood' and the acceptance of one flag 'will strongly foster the concept of a common fatherland, of a common love for and loyalty towards that fatherland, and the realization of a separate South African nationhood'.[2] This was language English-speaking South

---

[1] House of Assembly Debates, February 1, 1957, Vol. 93, col. 482. The speech is reproduced in D. W. Krüger, *South African Parties and Policies 1910–1960* (London, Bowes & Bowes, 1960), pp. 215–22.

[2] *Ibid.*, February 1, 1957, Vol. 93, col. 487. Also reprinted Krüger, *ibid.*, p. 220.

Africans found it hard to accept and harder to use.[1] Their position in a separate South African nation was that of a minority within a ruling minority. The British connection was based not only on sentiment; it provided some counterpoise to the majority, a psychological support on which to lean 'when Smuts goes'.[2]

Within little more than a generation of Union the former ruling European group thus found itself, while remaining socially and economically the most highly privileged in the Union, politically in a position of seemingly perpetual numerical inferiority in a unitary state, where there was increasing evidence that the ideal of unity was foundering on a resurgence of distinctive cultural consciousness. The soul of Afrikanerdom was an exclusivist soul, said Mr Strijdom in 1953. It had not been misled by the United Party which 'has always been the servant of the British Empire', it had not been denationalized by the policies of Botha, Hertzog and Smuts.[3] It was a republican soul, and so the independence 'which we visualize must end in a republic'. But what would be the place of English-speaking South Africans when that final goal of an Afrikaner republic was realized? 'We reject the idea entirely', Professor L. J. du Plessis had written earlier, 'that all South Africans should together be considered as one people. For us Afrikanerdom is the People of South Africa and the rest of the South Africans are, as far as

---

[1] G. Heaton Nicholls, *South Africa in My Time* (London, Allen & Unwin, 1961), in a chapter entitled 'The Inside Story of the Flag Act 1926-8', gives an illuminating account of how the two flags came to be adopted and the symbolic and emotional significance of the retention of the Union Jack to English-speaking South Africans at that time. He notes sadly there was no great public outcry in 1957 and comments that 'the Englishman in South Africa has largely lost his feeling for the roots which originally established him. . . . The Nationalist ideology is slowly and faithfully accomplishing its task' (p. 191).

[2] Such was the title of A. N. Keppel-Jones's book published in 1947 (London, Gollancz), which foreshadowed the consequences for English-speaking South Africans of Afrikaner Nationalist rule.

[3] *The Times*, September 23, 1953.

they are white, either potential Afrikaners or aliens.'[1] No one need take professors too seriously but English-speaking South Africans—unlike Englishmen—could hardly afford to disregard the implications of such professorial pronouncements altogether.

The Union was proclaimed on May 31, 1910, by the King's Representative, the Governor-General, Lord Gladstone, with little ceremonial because of the death of King Edward VII earlier that month; to mark its fiftieth anniversary, celebrated in a time of tension and with an air of constrained rejoicing, the Government of the Union of South Africa issued a crown piece but the coin for the first time did not bear an imprint of the Queen's head. 'It was not', explained the Minister of Finance Dr Dönges, 'considered appropriate for the occasion.' This trifling matter fairly indicates the transformation in the position of the English-speaking minority. Where once backed by the imperial power they imposed, and not always with good sense or good manners, their own symbolism on South Africa now they were watching the symbolism of the conquered republics coming into its own again. To the early period of the predominance of British monarchical symbols there succeeded the intermediate period of a dual symbolism: the period of dual citizenship, of the two anthems, the two flags and the two languages in effective equality,[2] and then in the latest period that in turn has given, and is giving, way perhaps ultimately even in respect of language to a single Afrikaner republican symbolism. The transformation has been gradual. For South Africans Commonwealth citizenship remained in diluted form after the enactment of the South African Citizenship Act in 1949, despite the prevailing Afrikaner view that 'clinging to a hyphenated citizenship blocks the establishment of an unhyphenated nation'.[3] South Africa remained a monarchy in name—though the Queen's title as proclaimed in the Union

---

[1] Quoted M. Roberts and A. E. G. Trollip, *The South African Opposition 1939–45* (Cape Town, Longmans, 1947), pp. 14–15.

[2] Curiously enough fully bi-lingual cheques, for which French-Canadians have pressed, were not issued in South Africa.

[3] Quoted Carter, *op. cit.*, p. 55.

in 1952 omitted the traditional phrase 'by the Grace of God' through no theological oversight—some years after it was one in fact. But what had happened was clear enough; the symbolism and more than the symbolism of the conquered had replaced that of the conqueror.

The proclamation of the republic, symbolically made close by Kruger's statue[1] in Church Square in the heart of Pretoria on May 31, 1961, was the last stage in the fulfilment of a purpose understood by Lord Selborne and pursued with a stubborn persistence over the years that compels admiration. That purpose was the undoing of the consequences of defeat in what General Hertzog used to speak of as 'the Second War of Independence'.[2] There was no concealment about the fundamental nature of the change in constitutional form. 'It would be a mistake', said Dr Verwoerd in outlining the plans of his Government for the holding of a referendum on the republic in 1960, 'for people to say that becoming a republic merely means that the Governor-General is now called the President.... It is the monarchy which is being replaced by a republic.'[3] The legacy of Kruger at the last proved stronger than the ideas of Milner, the influence of Hertzog and Malan greater than that of Botha and Smuts, Afrikaner nationalism than British imperialism, or to be more exact in respect of the last, Afrikaner nationalism than English nationalism in South Africa. For as an Afrikaner writer under-

---

[1] The correspondent of *The Times* (June 1, 1961) wrote that the statue of 'old President Kruger towered broodingly' over the scene, while *The Daily Mail* reported more dramatically that 'Paul Kruger, President of the old Transvaal Republic, stole the show with sinister, almost terrifying, effect. He towered, black and forbidding, a 40-foot high bronze statue in top hat, frock coat and stick, based in granite in Pretoria's Church Square.'

[2] In a speech in the Joint Session of Parliament on February 25, 1936, General Hertzog used both this phrase and 'the Three Years' War' to describe the South African War 1899–1902. It is reprinted in Krüger, *op. cit.*, pp. 385–92.

[3] House of Assembly Debates, January 20, 1960, Vol. 103, col. 104.

lined in the latest phase as British imperialism withdrew, there were left face to face two European nationalisms, 'two population elements with conflicting national ideals, one of which wanted to bring to fruition a South African nation with a national identity and national institutions of its own, and another which wanted to remain part of a British world nation and keep South Africa an integral part of a British World Empire.'[1] When the republic was approved by referendum on October 5, 1960, the Prime Minister, Dr Verwoerd, expressed the belief, despite all the evidence of the voting to the contrary, that the conflict of the nationalities had ended and that South Africans in consequence 'need never again feel like two nations in one state'.[2] Yet it was not in question that it was the Afrikaners who had prevailed in a struggle for predominance which had lasted one hundred and fifty years. And the reason why this was so was in the first instance their numerical superiority and in the second and at root the fact that Afrikanerdom for all its internecine feuds had a cohesion not to be found elsewhere in white South Africa. 'The Boers whatever their differences may be are in the last resort solidly fenced round by national and racial feelings. The others have about as much cohesive principle as chaff on a windy day.' So wrote Patrick Duncan in 1909.[3] Afrikaners thought in terms of race and culture, they spoke of the heart or soul of Afrikanerdom and they had a belief born of frontier isolation in their destiny and their oneness which explains why this beaten people came into their own, and more than their own again, leaving English-speaking South Africa to pay the price of English magnanimity and, be it added, their own political inertia. Fifty years had not seen the fulfilment of Campbell-Bannerman's or Botha's hopes of fusion. The state had not brought into being a nation—even a white nation. There remained union in name; distinct and self-conscious cultural

[1] W. van Heerden, 'October 5—End of a conflict of centuries'. *The Guardian*, October 5, 1960 (in translation from the Afrikaans).

[2] *The Times*, October 8, 1960.

[3] Quoted Thompson, *op. cit.*, pp. 178–9.

identities in fact.[1] The wounds of what the Englishman, Morley, termed the pirate war were not healed by what the Afrikaner, Botha, described as the magnanimous peace.

[1] It was officially estimated in 1960 that the home language of 56·9 per cent of the European population was Afrikaans, 39·4 per cent English, 2·3 per cent spoke other languages, and no more than 1.4 per cent were accustomed to using both English and Afrikaans as a home language. The last indicates the comparative infrequency of inter-marriage. See *Commonwealth Relations Office Handbook 1961*, p. 203.

THE PRICE FOR NON-EUROPEANS

> For the first time we are asked to write over the portals of
> the British Empire: 'Abandon hope all ye who enter here.'
> KEIR HARDIE
> House of Commons, August 16, 1908

The bearded Voortrekkers in their two ox-wagons who travelled slowly northwards from the Cape in 1938, one to the Blood River Battlefield and the other to the heights near Pretoria where a granite memorial now stands, were commemorating the centenary of the epic event in the history of Afrikanerdom—the Great Trek with its twin themes of survival in battle against native hordes and settlement of a hinterland conquered and held by the Boers alone. That Trek had been undertaken because the Boers, irked beyond endurance by the practices[1] and the humanitarian ideas of British colonial government, resolved to establish a society in which their conceptions of frontier life and especially their views of the proper relation between European and native should for all time prevail.

The Boers conceived that it was a part of the ordinances of God as set forth in the Old Testament that the African should serve the European and that the relation between them should accordingly be that of servant and master. This view was written into the constitution of the old South African Republic, where it was stated categorically that 'the people desire to permit no equality between coloured people and the white inhabitants of the country, either in Church or State'. This traditional

[1] There was one thing that appeared to the Boers perilously close to sharp practice—compensation for slaves in Government funds which soon afterwards sharply depreciated in value.

South Africa 1906–1961

Trekker conception of race relations has been passed down from one generation to another little questioned until recent times fundamentally, in the words of Professor C. W. de Kiewiet, because 'the withdrawal from the old Cape Colony meant that there was no party in the Republic with roots in humanitarianism or the philosophic optimism of the eighteenth century to soften the asperity of Voortrekker Calvinism'.[1]

The rigidly exclusive franchise of the South African Republic had its contrast and its counterpart in the Cape franchise with voting rights determined on a basis of property and civilization, not colour. If it was more liberal in principle than in practice, it derived none the less from a fundamentally different view of race relations. And continuing Boer suspicion of Britain was grounded in the belief that she was resolved to bring in, through Cape Colony, liberal humanitarian notions of race relations altogether alien to them. Cecil John Rhodes, with his enunciation on the eve of the War of 'equal rights for every civilized man south of the Zambesi', was giving renewed and, as it seemed, provocative support to ideas which were anathema to the Boers of the Northern Republics.

To Milner, and to the 'official' mind in London, the conflict of principle over the right view of race relations was a contributory cause, or alternatively a justification, for war. The natives themselves were led to suppose that a British victory in a conflict, the immediate occasion of which was a dispute about the rights of British subjects in the Transvaal, chief among them the wealthy uitlanders of Johannesburg, would greatly improve their lot, with the result that for the most part they were sympathetic to the British cause. This in turn added to the humiliation of defeat for the Boers,[2] for while they were honourably and inevitably overwhelmed in the end by the superior force of British arms, they suffered defeat in the sight of a people whom they deemed to be of a lower order of creation, whose sympathies had been enlisted against them and who expected to

[1] C. W. de Kiewiet, *The Anatomy of South African Misery* (Oxford, 1956), p. 23.   [2] *Ibid.*, p. 20.

THE PRICE FOR NON-EUROPEANS

profit from their overthrow. Sixty years later a Cabinet Minister in Dr Verwoerd's Government could explain the South African War in terms of the crushing of small republics by a mighty Empire intent not only on ending their separate existence but also on destroying Afrikaner political influence for ever by giving the vote to the natives in the former republican territories.[1] This nefarious plan was credited to Lord Milner, and on this view it was only the violence of the Afrikaner reaction that led to its abandonment. What substance is there in this interpretation? Certainly Milner, at least in his earlier phase, would have favoured an extension of the Cape liberal franchise to the northern provinces and would at all times have deemed it no disadvantage if this had undermined Boer predominance there, but such a policy was never adopted not because of the opposition of the Boers but because of the opposition of the great majority of the Europeans within South Africa. This Milner had recognized frankly before the war. He had written an admonishing letter to Asquith in 1898 saying: 'You have, therefore, this singular situation that you might indeed unite Dutch and English by protecting the blackmen, but you would unite them against yourself and your policy of protection. There is the whole crux of the South African position....'[2]

The Boers feared, and the natives hoped, that after the war the British Government would insist on extending the application of Cape Native policy to the northern provinces. In the event the fears of the Boers proved unfounded and the hopes of the natives were belied. Does this suggest that there is substance in the allegation, very different to that advanced by Afrikaners, that after the war native interests were sacrificed in order to unite the white races, not against but with the Imperial Government, or in the terms of Merriman's charge against Milner, in an attempt 'to reconcile the whites over the body of the blacks'?[3]

[1] Dr J. A. M. Hertzog, *The Times*, October 12, 1960.
[2] *Milner Papers*, Vol. I, p. 178.
[3] Quoted Thompson, *op. cit.*, p. 117. J. X. Merriman was Prime Minister of the Cape 1908–10.

It is important that this charge should be considered in its contemporary context. In that context we must remind ourselves first and once again that the thinking of the Imperial Government was dominated by what was called 'the Racial Question' and by which was meant relations between the two European peoples in South Africa. And it was dominated for the good reason that these white communities alone could at that time provide men locally who could assume responsibility for the Government of southern Africa. Though not without its difficulties, it was possible to think of the administration of the defeated republics with the co-operation of the defeated Boers, but was it possible to think of their administration *against* the Boers? Indeed, some spoke then, or have argued since, that instead of thinking in terms of the Durham Report the Imperial Government should have thought rather of India and administration by a South African Civil Service analogous to the Indian Civil Service. But in the face of stubborn Boer opposition and certain English-speaking resentment, this would have been a formidable undertaking indeed. It was one, moreover, altogether out of harmony with Liberal thinking about South Africa. 'Mr Chamberlain', reads a revealing note in Campbell-Bannerman's war-time papers, 'thinks we are strong enough for a military occupation of indefinite length and perhaps we are; but it is not the English way to govern white men as a subject race and England will be involved in a moral catastrophe, worse than all her losses, if we make the attempt.'[1] Here was an indication of a fundamental objection to the governing of white communities from London, even presumably in the interests of black. Radicalism was a more potent force than humanitarianism in early twentieth-century liberalism.

A second and more concrete point to be noted is that the British Government was bound in respect of native policy by Article 8 of the Treaty of Vereeniging. It read: 'The question of granting the franchise to natives will not be decided until after

[1] British Museum, Add. MSS. 41243A, f. 62. The note is undated but was presumably written in 1901 and probably used in a speech.

The Price for Non-Europeans

the introduction of self-government.' This was an explicit undertaking not to admit any native to the franchise in the Transvaal or the Orange River Colony while Britain had full control over them. It was an undertaking entered into by the Unionist Government and accepted by Milner without protest—even if to his subsequent regret. Once made, it was considered an obligation of honour. Certainly, it made reconciliation of Boer with Briton easier and, since this was the principal aim of the Liberal Government, they may be accounted fortunate that their hands were tied by their predecessors' action on this potentially most disruptive of questions. But that in no way lessens the responsibility of the Unionist Government and their entering into such an obligation in itself disposes of any pretension on their part to be regarded as the champions of native rights.

Article 8 of the Treaty meant that the position of the natives (and the Coloured, even though they were not specifically mentioned in the Article) continued to be more favourable at the Cape than in the northern provinces. This difference applied, and was understood in the Colonial Office to apply, to occupation and ownership of land and, above all, to electoral rights. There were a large number of native and Coloured voters on the rolls of Cape Colony, where as we have seen what was roughly a civilization franchise prevailed and where, incidentally, the passing of the Civilization Test carried for a native the right to purchase liquor—which explains the comment of one inspector of Native Locations to the effect that the harder the drinker, the more ardent his search for civilization. In the Transvaal and the Orange Free State, however, no kind of equality was admitted: there was no vote for native or Coloured inhabitants, and this continued to be not only a matter of practice (as it was, in effect, in Natal) but of clearly enunciated doctrine. To the natives and to the Coloured people the franchise was, as Lord Selborne reminded the Colonial Office,[1] 'a sign of admission into the civilized community' round which their hopes were centred. But while the franchise was psychologically most

[1] Selborne to Elgin, March 12, 1906. C.O. 291/97,

important to the educated natives, it was by no means the only respect in which non-Europeans received more favourable treatment at the Cape than elsewhere. At the Cape they were not debarred from any industry or profession, and they might, and did, own land as individuals. There was no Pass Law applied to Coloured people. But in both the Transvaal and the Orange River Colony, as Lord Selborne noted in the same despatch (which did not pass without critical marginal comment in respect of detail in the Colonial Office), natives might not own land and were excluded from all trade and skilled industrial work. In neither province might either the natives or the Coloured become burghers, and in both they were subject to Pass Laws. Moreover, continued Lord Selborne, 'speaking generally' it was hard for a native in the Transvaal to obtain justice as between himself and a white man in any circumstances, and the lash was applied with the utmost freedom to natives, not only by the officials but by the farmers. Otherwise their treatment on the farms was 'in general kindly'.

Lord Selborne observed, and in all the circumstances this is hardly surprising, that throughout the war the Coloured people were in the great majority enthusiastically on the side of the British, and that while many of the natives in the Transvaal remained faithful to their Boer masters, and the majority, who were 'almost all uneducated and uncivilized', remained watching the conflict without showing particular sympathy for either side, there was no question 'but that nearly every native throughout South Africa, who had made any strides towards civilization, was on the side of the British'. They were on the side of the British because the Coloured people and the educated natives at least believed that a British victory involving the annexation of the Transvaal and the Orange Free State would lead to an amelioration of their position in those provinces. It was these hopes, as Lord Selborne sadly reported four years after the ending of the war, which had been 'largely disappointed'. Certainly there had been improvements—'the random use of the lash' had been absolutely stopped, and the old Pass Laws remodelled. But even

The Price for Non-Europeans

here the beneficial consequences of the change were not felt to the extent they might have been because of the great difference between the British and Boer administration. 'The British here, as everywhere else, administer a law as long as it *is* a law. The Boers passed all kinds of laws, but administered them quite casually, and therefore it is probably true that the natives are more sensible of the administration of the Pass Law now than they were in the old days.' So also in respect of taxation, for while the tax was no higher under British rule, the collection of tax was no longer lax but strict, and its burden therefore more keenly felt. But it was not in respect of Pass Laws or taxes that Coloured and native disappointment was keenest. It was in respect of the franchise. They had hoped to enjoy the same position in the Orange River Colony and the Transvaal as they enjoyed in Cape Colony. This, in the High Commissioner's view, would have been neither possible nor wise, because the number of educated natives in the Transvaal and the Orange River Colony was very small. 'Moreover,' and here he touched on the heart of the problem, 'it was above all things necessary to prevent the Boers thinking that the British were going to put them on the same level as the natives or coloured people.'[1] The natives' disappointment, therefore, lay in the fact that in the terms of surrender it was promised that no franchise 'should be granted to Coloured people or natives unless granted by a legislature elected by the people'. They understood only too well what this condition meant, and to the natives and more particularly the Coloured people to whom the franchise was a flag, a sign of admission into the civilized community, the disappointment of their highest hope was great indeed. Yet what was the Liberal Government to do?

The Colonial Office files abound in statements of what an Imperial Government could *not* do. It could not go back on Article 8 of the Treaty. It did not feel that it could interpret that Article narrowly, applying it only to the natives because, as the West Ridgeway Committee reported, the Boers had in good faith

[1] *Ibid.*

interpreted it as applying to all non-European inhabitants and while the 'coloured' inhabitants of the country 'undoubtedly deserve much consideration' the Committee did not feel 'justified in putting upon the Agreement a different interpretation from that which is attached to it by the white population of both Colonies'.[1] The Secretary of State, Lord Elgin, who thought it quite evident that 'the time must come when there will be danger of a collision between the white and coloured races unless the relations between them are fair and equitable',[2] considered anxiously what steps might be open to the Imperial Government. But when the steps 'open to us to secure the just interests of the natives' were considered one by one, the objections to each seemed wellnigh insurmountable. The Secretary of State himself conceded that the terms of surrender 'absolutely preclude' representation of natives as in Cape Colony, and he thought it also excluded representation of Coloured people as well. He weighed the possibility of making reservations in the grant of the constitution, but noted that there would obviously be difficulty in framing any provision, and that quite certainly any such provision would be objected to. The root of the problem was to find a way in which the humanitarian aims of the Liberal Government towards the non-Europeans might be reconciled with their policy of generosity towards the defeated Boers in the form of restoring self-government to them. This was well understood and clearly stated. 'I am afraid', wrote Sir Montagu Ommanney, the Permanent Under-Secretary of State for the Colonies, 'that it is impossible to devise effectual means of controlling the native policy of a self-governing Colony' for 'when we decide to give that form of government ... where there is a large native population, we deliberately accept the risk of having to save the white community from the consequences of its mismanagement of the natives.'[3] And the Assistant Under-Secretary, Mr (later Sir) Frederick Graham, had already noted again with the same considerations in mind, 'We may by

[1] The Report is reprinted in C.O. 291/112. See also *African*, 840.
[2] C.O. 291/97, *loc. cit.*   [3] *Ibid.* Minute of April 7, 1906.

THE PRICE FOR NON-EUROPEANS

provisions in the new Constitutions prevent things from getting worse, but once Responsible Government is granted we cannot do anything towards making things better'. In sum, the Imperial Government, in the view of its advisers, was restricted to safeguards and a possible negative imperial veto. There was no way in which they could improve the lot of the non-Europeans consistent both with the terms of Article 8 of the Treaty and with their own policy of self-government for the Europeans. So much was realistically conceded, given the state of white public opinion in South Africa, on the native question, but one official at least felt strongly that, in view of the repeated representations which the British Government had made to President Kruger before the war about the treatment of natives in the Transvaal, it was not 'to our credit that so very little has been done....'[1]

The possibility of securing some concessions in respect of the treatment of natives in the northern provinces while the Imperial Government retained control and before responsible self-government was restored was not overlooked. Once it was decided, to quote a Colonial Office minute on this point,

'that we are to step straight from Crown Colony Govt. to Responsible Govt. the question assumes rather a different aspect and if anything is to be done [for the natives] it must be done before Crown Colony Govt. expires.'[2]

The difficulty, however, seems clear enough. Had they attempted to make the grant of self-government conditional upon the acceptance of a native policy more in accord with their liberal views, then the policy of the Liberal Government towards the Boers would have seemed neither generous nor magnanimous but rather as yet one more British attempt to impose ideas of race relations wholly antipathetic to Boer conceptions of what was at once right and practical. Once, however, the restoration of self-government was conceded without such conditions, then

---

[1] Minute of F. Graham, April 30, 1906, on Lord Selborne's despatch of March 26th. C.O. 291/97.   [2] *Ibid.*

greater confidence in British intentions was more than counterbalanced by the loss of her strong negotiating position. It is evident indeed that if, at this comparatively late stage, anything was to be done for the natives, the backing of the Imperial Government alone was hardly enough. What was required in addition was the support of some solid body of European opinion in South Africa. It was precisely this that was lacking. There is no greater illusion than to suppose that at this time English opinion outside the Cape—where the liberal tradition was cherished by Boer and Briton alike—was readily distinguishable from Boer opinion in regard to political or social rights for natives.

'However democratic whites in South Africa may be in respect of each other', wrote Lord Selborne, 'there is nothing in the world less democratic than the attitude of the white working man towards every black of any position or extraction.'

And he instanced in support of his contention a debate in the Johannesburg Town Council about natives riding in tramcars when,

'there was no more determined opponent to the admission of any native or coloured man to any part of a tramcar than Mr Whiteside, whose democratic principles towards his fellow whites are of the purest milk of the Australian labour word.'[1]

In such circumstances, any insistence by the Imperial Government on the application of their ideas, in however qualified a form, on social or political rights even for the comparatively small minority of educated natives would clearly have provoked the most violent reaction. Without exception the parties in the Transvaal were united in the view that they knew best how to deal with non-Europeans and a long memorandum on native policy written by Selborne at Botha's suggestion was likely, if anything, to have strengthened their conviction on this point[2]. On January 6, 1906, for example, the Transvaal Responsible Government Association stated:

'We hold that the people of the Transvaal are best qualified to legislate on questions affecting the coloured races in this Colony, and we submit

[1] Despatch of March 26th. [2] *African*, 897 (3907, p. 18).

that the specific reservation of such legislation for the decision of the Home Government may be the cause of regrettable conflict.'[1]

This conviction, recorded before the announcement of the intention to restore self-government, remained in the mind of the Transvaal political leaders of all parties as one of the principal gains to be secured when self-government was achieved. The Transvaal would have control of the native policy and this was something which the overwhelming majority of European Transvaalers were prepared in no circumstances to sacrifice. For the Imperial Government, therefore, there were risks either way. The Secretary of State, Lord Elgin, in considering the grant of self-government to the Transvaal and after it had been pointed out that the hands of the Imperial Government would be tied in respect of native policy, wrote 'It is better we should take the risk with our eyes open'.[2] In sum, therefore, the Imperial Government was much preoccupied with the native question. Its eyes were open but its hands were tied. This, it may be repeated, was not an altogether unfortunate circumstance for them especially since it was the Unionists who in this respect had tied them.

While nothing could be done before the restoration of self-government in respect of native rights, nothing could be done after because there was self-government. The debate in South Africa leading to Union made it abundantly clear that either there was Union with at most existing electoral laws in each colony, which meant an absolute political colour bar in the inland provinces and a nearly absolute political colour bar in Natal, or negotiations for Union broke down. The Cape was no more prepared to sacrifice its liberal franchise than the Transvaal or the Orange Free State were prepared to extend it to their own territories. There were individuals, W. P. Schreiner notable among them, who to their credit foresaw many of the consequences of compromise and protested at acquiescence in illiberal northern practices. They enjoyed, however, only

[1] Memorandum to Lord Selborne. C.O. 291/95.
[2] *Ibid.* Minute April 7, 1906.

qualified support within the Cape and lacked any solid backing elsewhere. The reaction to the draft constitution for Union was favourable in the Transvaal, reported Lord Selborne on February 15, 1909, six days after its publication. But he went on: 'There is no doubt that the Cape Native Franchise and Coloured franchise is not popular in this Colony.'[1] And General Botha on a tour of the Transvaal, again after the Convention had published its Report, had in fact great difficulty in preventing resolutions being passed for the removal of the Cape native franchise.

'I can assure you', he wrote to Merriman in Cape Town, 'that a very great number of people in the Transvaal, English as well as Dutch, are quite prepared to wreck the Union on this question.'[2]

This was something not to be lightly discounted. Union without the Transvaal was at once unthinkable and impracticable.

'It must never be forgotten', Mr Winston Churchill had noted in the files of the Colonial Office, 'that the politics of the Transvaal are the politics of South Africa.'[3]

That was something that neither the Convention nor the Imperial Government could afford to overlook.

Should Union have been wrecked on the question of the native franchise and the exclusion of non-Europeans from the Union Parliament? W. P. Schreiner certainly thought so.[4] Drawing on the experience of the years he warned Smuts in September 1908 not to risk, in youthful ambition, the building of a state upon unsound and sinking foundations. Freedom, he urged, but urged in vain, could not be real unless the natives had full opportunity to achieve equality. There was no room in South Africa for any that were not free and free to rise. A number of Radical and Labour Members of Parliament felt likewise but they preferred to evade the harsh choice before them

[1] C.O. 291/136.   [2] Quoted Thompson, *op. cit.*, p. 315.
[3] *African*, 817, January 30, 1906.
[4] See specially E. A. Walker, *W. P. Schreiner, A South African* (Oxford University Press, 1937), Chapter XIV entitled, 'A Blot on the Constitution'.

The Price for Non-Europeans

by thinking quite unrealistically of major concessions extracted by persuasion from London. Yet what was in fact the alternative to Union on the terms agreed in South Africa? It was not federation, for while federation would have afforded better safeguards for existing rights, enforcement of a colour-blind franchise on the northern provinces would have precluded federation as surely as it would have wrecked Union. It was the reimposition of imperial authority. In the mid-nineteenth century this was something that had been contemplated; by 1909 opportunity and conviction alike had gone. When the South Africa Bill came before a House of Commons which was thinly attended probably less because of lack of interest, as the South African Professor Thompson supposes, than because the grouse-shooting season had just begun, neither the Conservative Opposition nor the Liberal Government deemed imperial intervention desirable, let alone practicable. A. J. Balfour, who felt that the parties, however violently they had disagreed about South African affairs, were agreed that the white race should be dominant there, believed that

'the only glimmer of hope of dealing successfully with the real race problem in South Africa, is not to attempt to meddle with it ourselves, but, having made this Union Parliament, to trust the men of a like way of thinking as ourselves to rise to the occasion. . . .'[1]

Asquith, convinced that any interference from outside, particularly any interference from a distance, spasmodic, often ill-informed, and sometimes sentimental as almost certainly it would be

'is the very worst in the interests of the natives themselves',

concluded that the best chance of a satisfactory development of the native question would be when

'the problem is taken in hand, not by the several states individually and independently, but by a common body representing South Africa as a whole.'[2]

[1] House of Commons Debates, 1909, 5th series, Vol. IX, col. 1008.
[2] *Ibid.*, col. 1010.

SOUTH AFRICA 1906–1961

From confidence and strength might flow enlightenment. Such was the hope of a Liberal Prime Minister. Alas, it did not, perhaps at root because confidence was still lacking. White South Africa became, after Union, not less but progressively more obsessed with the fear of black numbers. But even if this were not so, a position of strength, as many Liberals were apt or preferred to overlook, allowed also, and even more obviously, of a tough, repressive native policy which would of itself cement European unity. That indeed had been one of the principal attractions of Union for English-speaking Natal, which had no liking for liberal Cape practices, as well as for the northern provinces. Lyttelton as Colonial Secretary had argued in March 1905 that greater caution in the direction of political change was necessary in South Africa than in Canada because of the native problem but Mr Churchill, who did not entertain the illusions of some of his colleagues, commented later that this view revealed 'a complete misapprehension' of the influence of the 'black peril' on South African politics.[1] It might indeed be a grave danger, 'perhaps—though remote—the gravest of all' but 'so far as the ... possibility of a native rising operates on the questions under discussion, it is a unifying force, perhaps the only unifying force, drawing the two white races together for mutual protection in spite of their animosities. ...' But at the time Mr Churchill wrote and later, it would cease to be such a unifying force, the moment one section of Europeans championed the cause of the natives. In 1909 such a time was evidently still far distant and indeed one Labour Member of the House of Commons thought it would never come. 'I am convinced', said Mr Ramsay MacDonald[2] in commenting on the exclusion by express provision of the South Africa Bill of non-Europeans from both Houses of the Union Parliament, 'from what I know from these men, what we know of the opinion of South Africa, that this bar is meant to be final, that it is not to be put in for the purposes of tiding

[1] January 2, 1906, *African*, 804.
[2] House of Commons Debates, 5th Series, August 19, 1909, Vol. IX, col. 1594.

The Price for Non-Europeans

over a temporary emergency. I am absolutely convinced that the intention of this provision in this Bill is that never, so far as man can secure "never", will the native, the coloured man, sit in the Parliament of United South Africa.' Was this a possibility that the Liberals and indeed the great majority in the House of Commons overlooked, unwisely discounted, or preferred to disregard?

The first was certainly not the case. The native question was the chief subject of the debates in the House of Commons. But in practice, though not in principle, the freedom of the House was limited by the knowledge that they were discussing a compact reached after protracted negotiation by the representatives of four self-governing colonies. 'The British Parliament', *The Annual Register*[1] records, 'did but register the compact between the respective governments. The Act therefore is the Act the South African Colonies wanted, not an Act shaped for them in whole or in part against their wishes by the Imperial Power.' Nor were the parts separable from the whole. When a Labour Member (Mr Barnes) proposed an amendment to remove the restriction in Section 26 of the South Africa Bill confining membership of the Union Senate to 'British subjects of European descent',[2] Asquith urgently appealed to the House not to wreck a great work of reconciliation. The passage of any such amendment carried not the risk, but the certainty of wrecking Union. Had the Imperial Parliament struck out the words 'of European descent' there would, as *The Annual Register* surmised at the time, 'have been no Act of Union'.[3] This was a prospect that induced restraint. It also encouraged a disposition, not unusual in such circumstances, to discount or disregard unpleasant

[1] *The Annual Register*, *1909*, p. 398.

[2] The Status of the Union Act, 1934 (S.6), amended Sections 26 and 44, which imposed a similar restriction on membership of the House of Assembly, of the South Africa Act, by deleting the words 'a British subject of European descent' and substituting 'a person of European descent who has acquired Union nationality'.

[3] P. 398. The commentary in *The Annual Register* is illuminating and well grounded.

realities on the part of many members. 'The temptation to hope for the best', remarked Dilke[1] who did not succumb to it, 'is so great that even many of us who have the greatest objection to this Bill establishing a rigid ineligibility of the natives are tempted to hope and believe against ourselves, and against our better reason, that things will go straight.' But when so much has been allowed for, the dominant fact remains that in 1909, and this can hardly be repeated too often, members were for the most part preoccupied with relations between the two European communities. Despite the warning of Schreiner from without, the admonitory address of the ageing Dilke, shadowed to the last by a lapse from the moral code which Victorian England could not forgive and Edwardian England could not forget, and despite the denunciations of Labour speakers, the great majority of members of the House of Commons and of the public remained unmoved, because this was not the question that seemed to them of first importance. R. C. K. Ensor, in his classic contribution to the Oxford History of England, entitled *England 1870–1914* and published in 1936, which by general consent most admirably reflects the spirit of the age of which he wrote, neither mentions Article 8 of the Treaty of Vereeniging[2] nor such criticism as there was of the neglect of native rights in 'the great national and imperial' achievement of Union.[3] It was indeed because that sense of a national and imperial achievement, transcending party allegiance and party record, was so pervasive that the harsh facts of non-European exclusion from all effective participation in the political life of the Union were glossed over with philosophic generalities or sanguine but, as it proved, ill-founded expressions of hope for future betterment. The

[1] House of Commons Debates, 5th series, August 16, 1909, Vol. IX, coll. 973–81 for Dilke's speech. This extract is from col. 974.

[2] See pp. 347–8, where the terms of the Treaty (including even that relating to the licensing of sporting rifles) are listed, with the notable exception of Article 8.

[3] *Ibid.*, pp. 390–1. Sir Robert Ensor was a member of the Fabian Society in its early days which makes the absence of any reference to the native problem the more striking.

The Price for Non-Europeans

quality of the achievement in this way served to obscure its gravest limitations. There was, however, solid and substantial, if not sufficient, reason why this should have been so.

The Liberal Government had not opened the way to Union in any such unquestioning spirit. Certainly they had regarded the reconciliation of the two Europen communities as the first aim of their policy, but the ways in which native rights might be safeguarded or extended had been carefully considered. There had been, however, and as we have seen, one overriding reason why nothing effective had been done—and it was one on which emphasis could not be placed in 1909 without reopening debate on the whole post-war settlement or implying mistrust of Boer intentions. It was the existence of Article 8 of the Treaty of Vereeniging which had deprived the Liberal Government of bargaining power at the first and vital stage on the road that led to Union. How they felt bound to interpret its letter and its spirit was summarized in the autumn of 1906, when a resolution of the Executive of the African Political Association was forwarded to London. It read:[1] '... since it is the intention of the British Government to enfranchise Whites only and since the 8th clause of Vereeniging only declared that the question of granting the franchise to natives will not be considered till after the introduction of self-government, His Majesty's Government is earnestly besought to lay down in the Constitution to be granted to the Transvaal that the franchise will be granted within a year by Letters Patent to coloured and natives unless they have been enfranchised during that period by the Colonial Government.' To this desperate plea came the inevitable rejoinder that: 'having regard to the interpretation generally placed upon the Vereeniging terms His Majesty's Government are precluded from prejudging the views of the future Government of the Transvaal by any reservation in the Constitution such as is proposed in the resolution.'[2] It was final; without breach of understanding, if not of faith, the reply could not

[1] Selborne to Elgin, October 31, 1906, C.O. 291/104.
[2] *Ibid.*, Elgin to Selborne, November 13, 1906.

have been otherwise and it afforded for some a welcome and for all a conclusive argument against any direct attempt to impose British views on racial policy upon the Transvaal or later upon the Union. That being so were not expressions of confidence in the new rulers of South Africa to be preferred to otiose regrets or idle threats?

The Imperial Government and Parliament did not feel, moreover, that they had to rely solely upon the reasonableness of men of like mind to themselves in the Union or the encouragement which a sense of security and strength might give to the enunciation of a more liberal native policy. The terms of the Treaty had removed the strongest weapon, but there were others left in the imperial armoury.

The architects of Union hoped that the three Protectorates of Bechuanaland, Basutoland and Swaziland would in due course be included within the jurisdiction of the South African Government. Two of these territories were enclaves within what was to be the Union of South Africa. The Liberal Government for their part consistently discouraged their native inhabitants from thinking that they could, or would, be excluded in perpetuity from Union rule. Thus on July 31, 1909, a petition from Basutoland for permanent exclusion from the Union elicited sympathy from His Majesty's Government which, however, could not contemplate 'that its government should remain permanently separate from that of the South African Union, by which it will be surrounded on every side'.[1] But equally the Imperial Government had no desire to precipitate events, and indeed as may be seen from the exchanges between the High Commissioner and the Colonial Office, their attitude in this regard was conditioned by the attitude of the Convention to the native franchise. The more liberal that was, the less stringent were to be the conditions for the transfer of the Protectorates.[2] But when it proved utterly uncompromising and particularly after the outright rejection by the Convention of all suggestion that

[1] Crewe to Selborne, July 31, 1909. C.O. 417/468.
[2] Crewe to Selborne, October 27, 1908. C.O. 417/459.

The Price for Non-Europeans

the franchise might be extended in any form to non-Europeans in the Transvaal, the Orange River Colony or Natal, the President of the Convention was told that it was the duty of the Government more than ever to 'secure ample safeguards for the Protectorates in the South Africa Act'.[1] This they did. In a Schedule to the Act, elaborate arrangements, to which much thought and attention had been given, were made to protect and preserve the position of the native inhabitants after responsibility for them had been transferred to the Union Government.[2] But the all important conditions related to the transfer itself. It was not to take place until the inhabitants of the territories had been consulted and the Parliament of the United Kingdom had assented. From this position no British Government, despite much pressure from successive South African administrations, has ever departed in any respect. On the one hand succeeding administrations have continued to insist to the Union Government that the inhabitants of the territories should be consulted before transfer and on the other they have declined to shift responsibility by making transfer conditional upon the assent of the inhabitants of the territories. Their stand has provoked outspoken criticism from the Union. In 1952 Dr Malan maintained that the failure to transfer these High Commission Territories was something that 'affects our equal status and place among the other members of the Commonwealth, as well as our self-respect as a nation'. And he went on to say that such a condition would not 'for a single moment be tolerated in their case, either by Canada or Australia or New Zealand, not to speak of India or Pakistan or Ceylon or Britain herself'.[3] But the

---

[1] The Cabinet also gave consideration to amendments to the South Africa Bill for the better protection of Asiatic subjects and to the administration by a Council, formed on the lines of the Indian Council of the Native Territories on July 16, 1909. See copy of Asquith's report to the King. Asquith Papers, Dep. 1. This would seem to be the only occasion when the Cabinet considered the implications of Union for non-Europeans within the Union itself at this time.

[2] Selborne to Crewe, November 6, 1908. C.O. 417/459.

[3] Mansergh, *Documents and Speeches*, Vol. II, pp. 921–9.

United Kingdom Government remained unmoved and, so far as the future can be foreseen, the importance of the High Commission Territories to the Republic of South Africa is likely not to diminish but to increase. However, at no time has it sufficed to persuade a South African Government to modify its native policies in order to secure the confidence or goodwill of the inhabitants of the territories. In so far as members of the Liberal Administration hoped that conditional exclusion of the territories would have this consequence, they were mistaken.

The other and particular safeguard of native rights was embodied in Section 35 of the South Africa Act. Its purpose also was defensive. It safeguarded the native franchise at the Cape. Like the other entrenched sections of the Act this section could be repealed or amended only by the special procedure laid down in Section 152 of the Act which itself could be neither repealed nor amended save by the procedure therein prescribed. This provided that no repeal or alteration of Section 152 or of the other entrenched sections of the Act would be valid unless the amending Bill was passed by both Houses of Parliament sitting together and was agreed to at the third reading by not less than two-thirds of the total[1] number of members of both Houses. Members of the Liberal Government, and notably the Secretary of State for the Colonies, Lord Crewe,[2] expressed great confidence in the effectiveness of this safeguard. In this they have been substantially justified. The Cape native franchise was in fact effectively safeguarded by the requirement of a two-thirds majority in a joint session, and its ultimate abolition was due not to the securing of that majority by the Nationalist Government, who in 1951 first introduced their Separate Representation of Voters' Bill designed principally to remove Coloured voters from the voting lists at the Cape, but by enlargement of

[1] The obstacle to amendment was the more formidable because of this insistence on a two-thirds majority not of those present and voting, but of the total membership of both Houses.

[2] House of Lords Debates, July 27, 1909, Vol. II, coll. 760-1.

THE PRICE FOR NON-EUROPEANS

the Senate so as to create an artificial two-thirds majority in both Houses sitting together.[1] If there was lack of foresight here it was rather on the part of the interested members of the Convention than on the part of the Liberal Government or its advisers.[2] The High Commissioner felt and the Secretary of State agreed that, failing a colour-blind civilization franchise test as the High Commissioner preferred, or an extension of the Cape franchise to the other provinces of the Union as the Secretary of State favoured, the existing Cape franchise should be entrenched in the constitution with a majority of three-quarters of both Houses of the Union Parliament sitting together required for its amendment. These views were communicated to the Chairman of the Convention where it was also proposed that the necessary condition for the abolition of the Cape native franchise should be a two-thirds majority in its favour in each House of the Union Parliament sitting separately, instead of both Houses sitting together. Had this latter device, the significance of which would not appear to have been fully grasped, been adopted then at least the Cape native franchise could not have been abolished by the Nationalist Government in 1955 simply by a temporary enlargement of the Senate. What the Liberal Government had failed to provide for was something altogether more far-reaching. It was the consequences within South Africa of the progressive decentralization of authority within the British Empire, to which indeed the Union itself gave a most powerful impetus. It was this process, culminating in the Statute of Westminster, 1931, which brought to an end the general reserve power of the Imperial Parliament over the Dominions and more particularly the overriding authority of Acts of the Imperial Parliament in respect of Dominion legislation.

[1] The Senate Act (No. 53, 1955) provided that the number of Senators should be increased from 48 to 90 and the number nominated from 8 to 10. When the purpose of this enlargement was achieved the number of Senators was reduced in the Senate Act, 1960, to 54.

[2] For the views of the High Commissioner see Selborne to Crewe, October 22, 1908, and for those of the Cabinet see Crewe to Selborne, October 27, 1908. C.O. 417/459.

South Africa 1906–1961

There is here a great paradox. In 1909, when the South Africa Act was enacted, any South African legislation repugnant to an Act of the United Kingdom Parliament was to the extent of such repugnancy null and void under the provisions of the Colonial Laws Validity Act, 1865. During and after the First World War this subordination of the Dominions in law was felt to be incompatible with new notions of equality as the root principle in imperial or Commonwealth relations and it was accordingly, and formally, terminated with the enactment of the Statute of Westminster in 1931. This legal endorsement of equality as the principle governing relations between Britain and the Dominions had in practice the incidental consequence of removing the imperial safeguard for the electoral rights of non-Europeans at the Cape. Liberal in intention it none the less undermined the one basically liberal provision in the South Africa Act.

So long as the Colonial Laws Validity Act was on the Statute Book the effective power of the Union Parliament to amend any of the entrenched clauses of the South Africa Act was slight since the measure of necessary agreement was difficult, if not impossible, to obtain. But once the Colonial Laws Validity Act was repealed by the Statute of Westminster and the legal sovereignty of the Union Parliament asserted in the Status of the Union Act, 1934,[1] the question arose whether the Union Parliament might not thereafter amend or repeal any section of the South Africa Act by simple majority or by any other procedure it saw fit to adopt. It was this question which was tested in the Courts subsequent to the passage through both Houses of the South African Parliament by simple majority of a Bill, the Separate Representation of Voters' Bill, 1951, to deprive non-Europeans of their franchise rights at the Cape. Before introducing the measure the Union Government sought and obtained legal advice, and not merely from their own Law

[1] No. 69 of 1934. Reprinted Mansergh, *Documents and Speeches*, Vol. I, pp. 4–6.

The Price for Non-Europeans

Advisers,[1] about the constitutionality of the proposed procedure. The advice they received encouraged them in their intended course. The essence of it, as stated by the Government's Law Advisers, was that since Section 2 (1) of the Statute of Westminster expressly provided that the Colonial Laws Validity Act, 1865, should not apply to any law adopted by the Parliament of a Dominion subsequent to the passing of the Statute of Westminster, it followed that Sections 35 and 152 (and the other entrenched sections) of the South Africa Act no longer involved any limitation whatsoever upon the legislative competence of the Union Parliament. They could be repealed or amended by that Parliament in the ordinary way without compliance with the requirements of Section 152 if its members so decided. In consequence of the passing of the Statute of Westminster the Union Parliament was 'the supreme and sovereign legislative authority in and for the Union' and 'it would accordingly be a negation of the sovereignty of the Union Parliament to say that Section 152 of the South Africa Act effectively prevented the Union Parliament from repealing or amending the provisions of that Section and of Section 35 in any other manner than the manner prescribed in Section 152, or that Section 35 binds Parliament to pass the laws therein referred to only in the manner therein prescribed'.[2] The Supreme Court rejected this view. The Judges, the majority of whom were Afrikaners, in their judgement on the validity of the Separate Representation of Voters Act, 1951, maintained that it was the South Africa Act, the terms and conditions of which were agreed to by the separate Parliaments of the four original colonies, that created the Parliament of the Union and not the Statute of Westminster, and that it was the South Africa Act also which prescribed the

[1] The opinion of Professor E. C. S. Wade, Downing Professor of the Laws of England at Cambridge University, is reprinted as Appendix II to Geoffrey Marshall, *Parliamentary Sovereignty and the Commonwealth* (Oxford at the Clarendon Press, 1957).

[2] *Opinion of the Government's Law Advisers on the amendment of the Entrenched Clauses in the South Africa Act.* Reprinted Mansergh, *Documents and Speeches*, Vol. I, pp. 91–7.

manner in which the constituent elements of Parliament had to function for the purpose of passing legislation. While the Statute of Westminster conferred further powers on the Parliament of the Union, it in no way prescribed 'how in the case of the Union legal sovereignty was divided between Parliament as ordinarily constituted and Parliament as constituted for the purpose of enacting certain amendments'. A state 'can be unquestionably sovereign although it has no legislature which is completely sovereign'.[1] It was this judgement which was circumvented by the enlargement of the Senate.

The elimination of non-European electoral rights at the Cape had been an objective of Afrikaners brought up in the northern tradition from the time of Union. It was attained after the major constitutional crisis in the history of the Union, in which once again the racial question in the strict sense of the term proved inseparable for the Nationalist Government, their supporters and indeed for many members of the Opposition, from the question of relations between the two European cultural groups. The South Africa Act was an Act of the United Kingdom Parliament. Did not the judgement of the Supreme Court in maintaining the supremacy of that Act, which was the Constitution of South Africa, imply that the Parliament of South Africa remained something less than the Parliament of a sovereign state? Did not this in turn suggest an element of subordination; of subordination of Afrikaners to a constitution which, though 'home-made', was nonetheless enacted as an Act of the Imperial Parliament? The opposition might distinguish between the written constitution of the Union and the unwritten constitution of the United Kingdom and state the consequences of that difference on the way in which sovereignty might be exercised. But no amount of constitutional argument or exposition served to dispel the suggestion of subordination.[2] It was this situation

---

[1] *Judgment of the Supreme Court on the validity of the Separate Representation of Voters Act* (No. 46 of 1951), March 20, 1952, reprinted *ibid.*, pp. 97–113.

[2] See House of Assembly Debates, May 6, 1952, Vol. 78, coll. 4911–5119.

The Price for Non-Europeans

which the Government, in the words of Dr Malan,[1] considered 'an intolerable one' and led to his insistence that it was imperative that the legislative sovereignty of Parliament should be placed beyond any doubt. Fortified by an impressive victory in the 1953 General Election, the National Party achieved its immediate aim without, however, freeing the South African Parliament from its subordination, at least in theory, to the constitution which brought it into existence. That only a republic approved by the people with a constitution enacted by the Parliament of South Africa could finally ensure. The native question and the European 'racial' question remained closely associated in 1961 as they had been in 1906.

Fifty years later, it can be very clearly seen that the basis of the Union was division and that the ultimate division expressed itself in the subordination of non-Europeans to Europeans. It was deemed to possess religious sanction. But it was not such subordination that many, if not most, of the leaders of the Dutch Reformed Church desired but separation—a separation which they believed carried with it a divine authority and which would mean in practice a more rigorous existence for Europeans dependent more upon their own exertions and less upon the labour of others. But the doctrine preached by high-minded theologians became corrupted in the politicians' market-place—so much so indeed that the doctrine itself was later presented in less absolute and more judicious phrases. 'The Dutch Reformed Church', stated a report on Race Relations published in 1956,[2] 'accepts the unity of the human race which is not annulled by its diversity. At the same time the Dutch Reformed Church accepts the natural diversity of the human race which is not annulled by its unity.' But such refinements of language did not suffice to impart to zealots a sense of humour or to rulers a sense of humanity. In the following year the Dutch Reformed Church withdrew its affiliation from the South African Temperance Alliance, and the National Chairman resigned because the alliance had 'introduced the un-South African principle of racial

[1] *Ibid.*, Vol. 78, coll. 3124–5. [2] *The Cape Times*, May 25, 1956.

integration and mixed gatherings' and therefore Afrikaner temperance workers had to find a new organization where they could keep 'their temperance principles without violating the Afrikaner's view of life and tradition'.[1] On the part of the rulers candour at least was not lacking. The policy, Mr Strijdom, the Prime Minister, proclaimed in recommending the Senate Bill in 1955 which, it will be remembered, was designed to ensure the necessary majority for the legislation removing non-Europeans from the Cape electorate roll, was the policy—which he maintained, with ample illustration from the speeches of his predecessors, was the traditional policy of the Union—that 'the White man should dominate'.[2] Mr. Strijdom was known as 'the Lion of the North'—a title once proudly borne by a Swedish king[3] who lies buried in the Riddarholm Church in Stockholm and before whose tomb, overhung with the captured flags of the Imperial Forces, a man may stand his heart still stirred by the memory of one who fought and died for what he conceived to be the rightful liberties of men. These are emotions Mr Strijdom's name is never likely to inspire. From the exclusion of non-Europeans from the Union Parliament, Keir Hardie foretold in 1909,[4] 'to rob them of the franchise is a very short and very small step'. Mr. Strijdom took it—and, if recorded words be any guide, with zestful enthusiasm.[5]

It was more than a step; it was an indication of a hardening resolve to reassert white supremacy at a time when it was crumbling elsewhere in Africa. The Africans who greeted Mr Macmillan in 1959 with the slogan 'We never had it so bad' knew what they were talking about. The intention of the Nationalist Government was not to end but to extend that

[1] *The New York Times*, April 14, 1957.
[2] House of Assembly Debates, May 23, 1955, Vol. 89, col. 6038.
[3] Gustavus Adolphus.
[4] House of Commons Debates, August 16, 1909, Vol. IX, col. 994.
[5] See his speech in House of Assembly Debates, Vol. 89, coll. 6031-50, where there is also a restatement of the constitutional question as seen by the Nationalist, or as they themselves preferred to be styled the National Party.

division which was at the foundation of Union. The *Bantustan* legislation, the significance of which may have been much underestimated, not only by the world outside South Africa but by the African leaders themselves, enunciated in effect a two, or more, nation theory. If it be the case, as one Afrikaner writer has urged,[1] that many people think wrongly of the South African problem in terms of groups of individuals and not of nations; if it is even partly true, as he also and further claims, that the advocates of a common society in the Union, obsessed with the idea that the Bantu is merely an uneducated Afrikaner or Englishman, fail to observe that not only is he neither, but that he is not even part of one homogeneous Bantu nation but a Zulu, or a Xhosa or a Sotho, and as such a member of an identifiable nation in its own right, then, if European or Asian history be any guide, the enunciation of a two, or more, nation theory foreshadows the break up of the existing multi-national state. There have been notable instances in European history in which the state has created the nation but at no time, and least of all at a time when African nationalism is in the ascendant, is it conceivable that the Republic of South Africa can create a single nation of three million Europeans and ten million Africans, the more so since both ruling minority and subject majority are themselves divided.

When the 'promotion of Bantu Self-Government Bill', 1959, was introduced, the Union Government spoke of it as an unequivocal assurance of its intention to create self-governing Bantu national units. If and when these units showed the ability to reach the required stage of self-sufficiency they would, in the Prime Minister's own statement, form a South African Commonwealth together with white South Africa which, so he hoped, would serve as its core and as the guardian of these emerging Bantu states. The contemporary reality is rigorous dependence; the ultimate goal professed to be partition and independence. Bitter preoccupation with practice inevitably precludes much

[1] S. Pienaar and Anthony Sampson, *South Africa, two views of separate development* (London, O.U.P., 1960), p. 9.

attention to principle within the Union; at a greater distance, however, it can be seen that the principle of partition has been enunciated and the phrases of independence employed. One day the Africans will surely seize upon them. They will not receive—they will demand—their Bantustans with frontiers very different from those laid down in the Bantu Self-Government Act, and on that day the future of the High Commission Territories will no doubt be resolved. In South Africa one beaten people has come into its own again. Is the day far distant when others will emerge from the shadows to insist their hour, too, has come round at last?

4

PRICE AND REWARD

> Magnanimity in victory is rare, and this is an instance and almost unique example of its reward, because rare though it be it is by no means always rewarded. W. S. CHURCHILL
> House of Commons, 1950

The title and in some measure the theme of this book might suggest that British magnanimity in South Africa exacted no price from the United Kingdom. Such, however, is not my contention. It involved the abandonment of direct British control over the policy, economy and wealth of the Union even though in respect of the latter it was rightly assumed that informal would long survive formal empire. But it is suggested that for the United Kingdom it was not a continuing, nor for its citizens a personal, price. It was not the survival of their political symbols, the status of their language, the education of their children that was going to be imperilled if the policy failed, nor were they likely to be immediately or individually affected if repressive native policies led at the last to violence or catastrophe. In these circumstances it is not surprising that for long British Commonwealth and indeed much South African opinion has been conscious less of the price than of the rewards of magnanimity in South Africa. 'There never was a revolution so wonderful and apparently so miraculous', wrote *The Manchester Guardian*, contrasting Union with the war that had so shortly preceded it.[1] Such views may have been too lightly and too

[1] *The Guardian*, May 31, 1960, quoting from *The Manchester Guardian*. The comment was written after the First World War.

hastily formed but we in our generation should beware of discarding them too lightly in turn. South Africa is a microcosm of many of the problems that vex the twentieth-century world: to draw up a balance sheet on imperial policy in South Africa is for that very reason an exacting exercise in historical accountancy. The opinion of our time is no more final than that commonly entertained by earlier generations.

From the time of Union until very recently, British opinion has indeed been much more conscious of the rewards than of the price of magnanimity in South Africa. Some of the reasons for this are psychological, others more material. Milner complained of the way in which the Liberals were continually harping on 'Boers, Boers, Boers':[1] but the fact was that the conscience of the nation was troubled about them. The great majority who believed at the time that the war was not discreditable, for the most part found it hard to persuade themselves, and even harder to persuade others, that it was creditable. While it was waged by the general agreement of both sides in an examplary manner by the forces in the field, it was associated at home, and especially in London, with brittle popular judgements and outbursts of mass hysteria which at the time some, and in retrospect most, Englishmen found it distasteful to contemplate. 'You can hardly imagine', wrote James Bryce, an experienced political analyst after all as well as a party politician, to Goldwin Smith in Toronto in April 1901, 'the moral and political declension of England at this moment. It will, I hope and trust, soon pass: ... Even among Radicals, even among the Non-conformist leaders, clerical and lay, the old ideals of justice, liberty, humanity . . . seem to have become obscured. Scarcely an attempt to realize the passion for independence which animates the people of these Republics; little recognition even of their tenacious courage. Disraeli's influence was bad enough; but one is amazed to find one's self wishing for Disraeli instead of those who now direct the Jingo whirlwind.'[2] A generous peace

[1] See above, pp. 42–3.
[2] H. A. L. Fisher, *James Bryce* (London, Macmillan, 1927), Vol. I, p. 317.

crowned by a dramatic gesture of confidence and goodwill towards the Boers restored, and alone could have restored, at home and more important throughout the Empire, the image of an England which, cherishing its faith in the government of men by themselves, was ever foremost in extending what it believed to be the supreme political privilege of self-government at least to the European peoples under its rule. Psychologically, therefore, self-government in a united South Africa was satisfying beyond the limits of party allegiance—so satisfying indeed that Lord Crewe, introducing the Second Reading of the South Africa Bill in the House of Lords, thought it worth while to emphasize the more robust faith in the virtues of self-government, displayed by the Liberal administration, in comparison with its Unionist predecessor and to allude with some professed amusement and regret to what he deemed to be unfounded Unionist fears lest an undue share of the credit for the Act of Union should be claimed by members of that administration, to whom nonetheless he believed it almost wholly belonged.[1] But, and this explains much, the satisfaction shared by Liberal,[2] Unionist, Irish Nationalist, though not by Labour,[3] Members derived directly from the sense that a settlement more generous than the circumstances demanded had been made with the Boers. In so far as Britain was felt in retrospect to have been less than just to them before or during the war, so for conscience' sake she had to be more than just to them after the war. Milner, a great administrator, whose life abroad and later at home was filled with miscalculations about the responses of his fellow-countrymen, believed in 1899 that by forcing differences with the Dutch republics to the point of war he would secure, among

[1] House of Lords Debates, July 27, 1909, Vol. II, coll. 755–6.

[2] The complacency of some Liberals exceeded all reasonable bounds, e.g. some egregious comments of the Parliamentary Under-Secretary of State at the Colonial Office, Colonel J. E. B. Seely, who should have known better, in House of Commons Debates, August 16, 1909, Vol. IX, col. 1598.

[3] See especially the speech by J. Ramsay MacDonald, *ibid.*, col. 1594, referred to above, pp. 74–5.

other things which admittedly he valued more, a better life for the natives under their jurisdiction. In the event he, and those who thought with or were persuaded by him, succeeded only in ensuring that reconciliation with a small defeated white community in South Africa would assume an assured precedence over the humanitarian claims of the large native majority. It was because Liberal magnanimity promised reconciliation with the Boers that most British people were psychologically prepared to think first of all of its rewards and only then, if at all, of its price.

There were also more substantial, though not necessarily more important, reasons for continuing to think of the South African settlement chiefly in such terms. With the transfer of power first to the Transvaal and the Orange River Colony and then to the Union went responsibility for trying to settle many troubles which filled the Colonial Office files in the early years of the century. If indolence is indeed a necessary ingredient of statesmanship, then British policy from 1906 onwards was not lacking in it. But, more positively, there was an imperial or Commonwealth aspect to Campbell-Bannerman's South African policy which made a deep and lasting impression on British thinking about it. The South African settlement was effected in the period of that final grouping of the Powers in Europe which portended an early struggle for supremacy between them. The year of the South Africa Act was itself the year of the Bosnian crisis, the most dangerous of all those which preceded the outbreak of the First World War. The Cabinet, as the Prime Minister's daily reports to the King abundantly testify, was preoccupied with problems of foreign policy.[1] Was it not a major act of statesmanship to have established a strong and friendly government in South Africa before the War came? And when it did, was there not a more striking vindication of the far-sighted wisdom it displayed? In August 1914 General Botha, Prime Minister of the Union, suppressed a rebellion among his own people and then led South Africa side by side

[1] Asquith Papers.

with the other Dominions of the Crown into the war against Germany. In that day not only the British people but the whole world, in the pardonably sweeping phrase of Campbell-Bannerman's biographer, judged Campbell-Bannerman's act of faith to have been splendidly justified. Nor was that all. During the war the people of the Transvaal, to whose political immaturity a Colonial Office official had so slightingly alluded in 1906, produced in Generals Botha and Smuts two of the outstanding personalities of the Imperial War Cabinet of 1917. Gallant leaders of a small defeated people reconciled to and eminent in the service of the Empire that had conquered them—that was a theme rare enough in the annals of history seemingly to justify in itself the policy which had led to it. 'My experience in South Africa', said General Smuts in 1919,[1] 'has made me a firm believer in political magnanimity and ... Campbell-Bannerman's great record still remains not only the noblest but also the most successful page in recent British statesmanship.' Here indeed he touched upon the heart of the matter. The policy was at once magnanimous and successful. Therein lay its almost irresistible appeal to the British people.

Such appeal was, however, by no means confined to the people of Britain. On the contrary subject peoples throughout the Empire saw, and rightly saw, in the policy a source of hope for the future. In giving self-government first to provinces and then to a state in which people of non-British extraction were in the majority the Liberal Government had transcended Durham, crossed the great divide and opened the way to a Commonwealth in which British majority nations were a minority of the total membership. A principle was established from which there was to be no going back, something of which present-day critics of the policy appear altogether oblivious. Yet in 1909 even the native leaders in South Africa showed awareness of the implications of the policy. They did not condemn it; they petitioned for the same generosity to be shown to them as had been shown to the Boers by the British Government. In April 1909 the South

[1] S. G. Millin, *General Smuts*, Vol. II, p. 211.

African Native Convention passed a resolution entering their 'strong and emphatic protest' at the nature of the colour bar to be imposed in the Union, which then went on to say that while the Imperial Government had honourably fulfilled 'its liberal promises' to the defeated republics, the natives and Coloured subjects of His Majesty 'have not been shown the same liberal and generous treatment' despite assurances that His Majesty's Government would not purchase peace at their expense.[1] But, as in the circumstances was to be expected, it was not on the natives in South Africa but on subject and more politically self-conscious peoples elsewhere in the Empire that the new departure made its deeper impression.

From 1906 onwards the records of the Indian National Congress abound in references to what had happened in South Africa and to the conclusions which the British people might reasonably draw from the encouraging consequences of their policy there. Despite oft-repeated disappointment that the Imperial Government had failed to use its 'persuasiveness and moral influence' to secure, as Indians believed it could have secured, the rights of British citizenship for Indian settlers in South Africa, the predominant reaction was one of envy and hope. An Empire that had been generous to one subject or conquered people might well be so to another. That faith in the freedom loving instincts of the English people to which constitutional nationalists were committed, and which had been so rudely shaken by the Boer War, was largely restored. 'The cases of the French in Canada', said G. K. Gokhale, the leader of the Moderates within the Indian National Congress in February 1907, 'and the Boers in South Africa showed that there was room in the Empire for a self-governing India.'[2] 'Self-government', S. N. Banerji told members of the Indian National Congress at their meeting in 1914[3] when the memory of de Wet and de la

---

[1] *African*, 927. Encl. to despatch from Selborne to Crewe, April 5, 1909, No. 65 (13915). [2] G. K. Gokhale, *Speeches* (Madras, 1916), p. 782.
[3] *Report of the Proceedings of the Twenty-ninth Indian National Congress*, 1914, p. 102.

Price and Reward

Rey's rebellion against the Union Government was fresh in mind, 'is the cement of the Empire. We appeal to the Government to give it to us, because it will lay broad and deep the foundations of British rule upon the contentment, happiness and gratitude of the people. We have had recently an object lesson, very cogent and very convincing. There was a rebellion in South Africa led by some of the malcontents. I put it to you. Would General Botha have been in a position to stem the surging tide of that revolutionary movement if he had not behind him the great body of people won over to the British connection by the inestimable boon of self-government?' S. N. Banerjea returned to the same theme and some of the same phrases when the Congress met in historic session in 1916[1] at Lucknow where Mrs Annie Besant declaimed: 'Where will you find a civilization worthy of freedom, if India be not worthy to be free? (Applause.) It is not as though it were a young nation, a mushroom nation, like the Boers in South Africa. If they, having fought against England, were worthy of self-government shall not you who are fighting beside her, claim self-government?'[2]

The argument was developed also by Pandit Jagat Narain. 'South Africa', said Narain,[3] 'is the latest example within the British Empire of the benefits of self-government. Undeterred by opposition in Parliament and the wailings of "the men on the spot", the Government of Sir Henry Campbell-Bannerman conferred full responsible government in 1906 and 1907, respectively on the Transvaal and the Orange River State [Colony], which less than six years before had been engaged in a bloody struggle with England. . . . The rivalries of race and

[1] *Report of the Proceedings of the Thirty-first Indian National Congress*, 1916, p. 75.   [2] *Ibid.*, p. 107.

[3] *Ibid.*, p. 8. Pandit Jagat Narain was Chairman of the Reception Committee and the extract is from his opening address. He dealt more fully with Canadian but more forcibly with South African precedents. Jehangir Bamanjee Petit (p. 92) suggested that the chief lesson to be drawn from South Africa and other colonies was the necessity not merely to tickle the British lion as Indians were doing but twist his tail and to rouse him to a sense of his responsibilities.

language, instead of finding free play, have as a consequence become less prominent than they were a decade ago, and the Dutch, so far from rising against England at the first favourable opportunity that offered itself, have been so completely won over by the magnanimous policy followed by her that they are today fighting side by side with her sons for the maintenance of the Empire.' 'She wiped from their brow the stigma of defeat and gave them [the South African republics] self-government,' said B. C. Mitter at the Calcutta Conference of the All-India Moderate Party in 1919, 'and ample has been England's reward. Rebellious foes have been converted into staunch supporters of her imperial system.'[1] While Indian Nationalists thus retold the tale and pointed the moral for the Imperial Government, implicit in their argument was the conviction that experience in South Africa had shown that the British Government and people had a genuine belief in self-government, that duly encouraged they would extend it to others under their rule and that therefore the reliance of the extremists on violence was at once ill-advised and unnecessary.[2]

This was also the theme of John Redmond, the last effective leader of the Irish Parliamentary Party, a man who aspired to fill the role of an Irish Botha, and who time and again appealed in private[3] or in public to the Liberal Government to pursue the same policy of trust and magnanimity towards Ireland as they had shown towards South Africa. But this in full measure was never forthcoming and as Redmond's life moved towards its tragic close he had to be content with specious references by Lloyd George to South African precedents when he decided all too late to call a Convention in May 1917 as the best hope of 'composing the unhappy discords which have so long distracted

[1] *Report of the Proceedings of the Second Session of the All-India Conference of the Moderate Party*, December 1919.

[2] Dr S. R. Mehrotra, Assistant Professor in History at Saugor University, has given me help in assessing Indian reactions which I am happy to acknowledge.

[3] John Redmond's papers in the National Library in Dublin provide the evidence for this statement.

Ireland'.[1] Yet though the constitutional movement expired with that Convention, the path that led through violence to the Anglo-Irish Treaty of 1921 was made the more acceptable to members of the Coalition Cabinet by the recollection, stimulated by the presence of General Smuts in London, of the success of the daring experiment of giving self-government to a nationally conscious people in South Africa fifteen years earlier. First in Ireland and then in India the rewards of magnanimity in South Africa prompted British statesmen to think of a national solution to the problem of relations with self-conscious national communities within the Empire.

Three of the signatories of the Anglo-Irish Treaty, Austen Chamberlain, Winston Churchill and Lord Birkenhead—the first of whom had voted against responsible self-government for the Transvaal in 1906 and the other two in favour, despite the claims of party allegiance in the case of the young F. E. Smith—defended their signing of that Treaty on the ground of the success of Britain's South African policy, though doing so moved Birkenhead to say to Michael Collins 'I may have signed my political death warrant'.[2] Austen Chamberlain, the son of the man who, in the Irish view, had killed Home Rule in 1886, earlier told a highly critical Unionist Conference in Liverpool of the reasons for his conversion to self-government for Ireland. There were, he said, after nearly thirty years in Parliament only one or two votes he had given that he would wish undone. One of them was the vote he had cast against the restoration of self-government to the defeated Dutch republics.

'By a great act of daring faith, they [the Liberal Government] conferred upon our recent enemies in the Transvaal and the Orange Free State on the morrow of our victory, full self-government. I voted against them. I thought it a rash and wicked thing to do. If we could have seen further into the future, if I could have voted in that division

[1] Letter from Mr Lloyd George to Mr J. Redmond, May 16, 1917, reprinted, Cd. 9019, pp. 50–1.
[2] Michael Collins's reflection was more evidently true: '... early this morning I signed my death warrant.'

with the fuller knowledge I have to-day, I should have known that that great act of faith was not, as I thought it, the destruction of our policy, but its completion and its fulfilment. That is the vote that I would undo if I could undo a vote once given. That great act, that daring act of faith, led directly to the reconciliation of the races in South Africa: it led to the Union of South Africa: it brought South Africa into the war with us.'[1]

And in the subsequent debate in the House of Commons on the Irish Treaty, Churchill, after acknowledging to the diehard critics of it that South Africa provided no exact parallel, went on: 'but surely it would be very foolish for us to cut ourselves off from the encouragement and inspiration which we may naturally and legitimately derive from studying the most adventurous and modern instance of trust and conciliation which the annals of the British Empire records!'[2]

In India, Irish experience was paralleled. In the Second World War, Mahatma Gandhi used the same arguments as Redmond had used twenty-five years earlier and to an unresponsive Viceroy. But while Congress pleas were disregarded at the time, again when a final settlement came to be made, those who made it appealed to the South African precedent. In 1947, Mr Attlee, moving the India Independence Bill, recalled that this was the second time in a generation that Britain had voluntarily abdicated her power over a dependent people, and argued that the nearest parallel to the action the Labour Government was then taking was Sir Henry Campbell-Bannerman's 'great act of faith' in 1906, an act which bore fruit in 1914 and 1939 and which he had often heard General Smuts describe as marking the end of imperialism.[3] When Mr Macmillan returned from his tour of independent or soon to be independent African states in 1960, he said with reassurance for the anxious, 'We have travelled this road before'.

---

[1] Sir Charles Petrie, *The Life and Letters of the Right Hon. Sir Austen Chamberlain* (London, Cassell, 1939), Vol. II, pp. 166–7.

[2] House of Commons Debates, December 15, 1921, Vol. 149, col. 183.

[3] *Ibid.*, July 10, 1947, Vol. 439, col. 2441.

Price and Reward

For British statesmen responsible for a transfer of power first to Ireland, then to India and later still to states in Africa or elsewhere, South Africa afforded at most a reasonable ground for sanguine expectation, at least a precedent which would invest policies that might otherwise be condemned as leading to the dismemberment of Empire with an air of traditional respectability. And in so far as it did this, the Liberal experiment in South Africa may be taken as a great divide marking off the idea of a *British* Empire from that of a community of many nations. Without Union there might have been no Commonwealth. If so much be even in part accepted, then here the last word may not unfittingly rest with Mr Winston Churchill, Under-Secretary of State for the Colonies and spokesman for the Colonial Office in the House of Commons in 1906, who, paying tribute to the memory of General Smuts forty-four years later, said: 'no act of reconciliation after a bitter struggle has ever produced so rich a harvest in goodwill or effects that lasted so long upon affairs.'[1] But what is substantially true of the Commonwealth is not of South Africa. There is clear reason for this. The Liberals in 1906-9 well understood the emerging strength of Dominion nationalism but in so far as they identified Afrikaner nationalism with Canadian nationalism they were guilty of oversimplification. Afrikaner nationalism was real and it was a stronger force than Canadian nationalism at that time. But over and above Afrikaner nationalism there was Afrikaner imperialism. It was the pastoral imperialism of the frontier, paternalistic in outlook and maintained not by the outward use of force but by the imposition of Pass Laws and the free use of the lash. Because of its frontier simplicity its capacity for survival, if not its very existence, passed almost unrecognized in the great metropolis of a twentieth-century Empire. Yet even here there is paradox and contradiction. The people whose subject status was more firmly riveted upon them in 1909 might find some cause for satisfaction and of hope for the future in the thought that, partly at least because of Union, statesmen from Asian and

[1] House of Commons Debates, September 13, 1950, Vol. 478, col. 1100.

African as well as European Commonwealth countries in 1961 considered together as equal partners, and pronounced against a South African republic's continuing Commonwealth membership on the ground of that racial segregation which was the basis of Afrikaner imperialism in South Africa.

It is unrealistic to think of balancing the price of magnanimity against its rewards. But it is equally unrealistic to consider the one without the other, to think only in terms of the price as is fashionable today or only in terms of the reward as was general yesterday. The consequences of the Liberal 'act of faith' in South Africa were far reaching and they are to be assessed in their Commonwealth as well as in their domestic setting. The state it helped to bring into being has had about it, despite the problems and tensions that threaten to overwhelm it, elements of greatness and it has by example greatly influenced events elsewhere. Those who fashioned it may now seem in some respects selfish, in others generous; in some ways naïve, in others far-sighted; but at root it was not they who failed so much as those who came after them who failed them. For, as Francis Bacon long since noted, that which men change not for the better, Time, the Great Innovator, changes for the worse.

INDEX

African National Congress, 36
African Political Association, 77
Anglo-Boer co-operation, 15–16, 20–2, 25 n. 1, 32–3, 38–64, 74–7, 84–5, 91–2, 95–6, 98–9
Anglo-Irish Treaty (1921), 97–8
Annual Register, The, 75
Asquith, H. H. (1st Earl of Oxford and Asquith), 28 n. 1, 29 n. 1, 31, 34, 36, 46, 63, 73–4, 75, 79 n. 1
Asquith Papers, 34 n. 1 and 2, 36 n. 2 and 3, 37 n. 1, 46 n. 3, 79 n. 1, 92 n. 1.
Attlee, C. R., 98
Australia, 26, 35, 38, 54, 76, 79

Bacon, Francis, 100
Balfour, A. J. (Earl of), 18–19, 21, 73
Banerjea, S. N., 94, 95
Bantu, 32–3, 36, 87–8
Bantustan, 87, 88
Barnato, Barney, 39
Barnes, G. N., 75
Basutoland, 78–80
Bechuanaland, 78–80
Beit, Alfred, 39
Besant, Annie, 95
Bloemfontein, 35
Bloemfontein Conference (1899), 27
Blood River Battle (1838), 61
Bond, Afrikander, 48
Borden, Sir Robert, 13
Bosnian Crisis (1908–9), 92
Botha, General Louis, 17, 22, 25 n. 1, 31, 36, 44–5, 47, 52–3, 56, 58–60, 70, 72, 92–4, 96
Broederbond, 50 n. 1
Bryce, James, 90

Bülow, Prince B. von, *Die Grosse Politik der Europäischen Kabinette 1871–1914*, 33 n. 1

Campbell-Bannerman, Sir Henry, 16–18, 20–3, 25, 26 n. 3, 27–31, 33–4, 38, 41, 50, 59, 64, 92–3, 95, 98
Campbell-Bannerman, Lady, 23
Campbell-Bannerman Papers, 21 n. 3 and 4, 25 n. 3, 29 n. 2, 64 n. 1
Canada, 26–7, 29, 35, 38–9, 51, 54, 57 n. 2, 74, 79, 94, 95 n. 3, 99
Cape Colony, 31, 35, 38–9, 44, 48, 61–3, 65–8, 70–2, 74–5, 79–84
Cape Times, The, 85 n. 2
Carnarvon, 4th Earl of, 33
Carrier, N. H. (and J. R. Jeffery), *External Migration 1815–1950*, 32 n. 1
Carrington, Lord, 28
Carter, G. M., *The Politics of Inequality, South Africa since 1948*, 45 n. 1, 57 n. 3
Ceylon, 32, 79
Chamberlain, Sir Austen, 97
Chamberlain, Joseph, 29, 33, 40–1, 64
Churchill, W. S., 25–7, 30, 34–5, 46–9, 72, 74, 89, 97–9
Collins, Michael, 97
Colonial Laws Validity Act (1865), 82–3
Colour bar, 70–1, 74, 94
Coloured people, 32, 65–8, 75, 77, 80, 94
Commonwealth (British), *see also* Empire, 15–18, 35, 53–4, 79, 82, 89, 92–3, 98, 100; (South African), 87

Crewe, 1st Earl of, 15–16, 35, 78 n. 1 and 2, 79 n. 2, 80, 81 n. 2, 91, 94 n. 1
Cruise O'Brien, Conor, *Parnell and his Party*, 23 n. 2

Daily Chronicle, The, 34
Daily Mail, The, 58 n. 1
Davitt, Michael, 38
Decentralization, of imperial authority, 52–3, 81, 93–9
De Kiewiet, C. W., *The Anatomy of South African Misery*, 62
De la Rey, General J. H., 44, 94–5
De Villiers, Sir Henry (Lord), 43
De Wet, General C., 44, 94
Dilke, Sir Charles W., 76
Dillon, J., 41 n. 2
Disraeli, Benjamin (Earl of Beaconsfield), 33, 90
Dominions (British), 15, 38, 41, 81–3, 93, 99
Dönges, Dr T. E., 57
Du Plessis, Professor L. J., 56
Duncan, Sir Patrick, 51, 59
Durban, 35, 43, 49
Durham, 1st Earl of, 28–9, 39
Durham Report, 64, 93
Dutch Reformed Church (*see also* Predikants), 44, 85

Eckstein, Hermann, 39
Edward VII, King, 17, 28, 36, 57, 79 n. 1, 92
Elgin, 9th Earl of, 24 n. 2, 26 n. 3, 34, 44, 46 n. 4, 47 n. 1, 49 n. 1, 65 n. 1, 67 n. 1, 68, 71, 77 n. 2
Empire (British), *see also* Commonwealth, 15, 17–18, 30, 36, 40–1, 48, 54, 56, 59, 63, 89, 91, 93–9
Ensor, R. C. K. (Sir Robert), *England 1870–1914*, 17 n. 1, 76
Entrenched Clauses (of South Africa Act, 1909), 49–50, 80–4

Fabian Society, 76
Federation, 27, 33, 38–9, 51, 73
Fisher, H. A. L., *James Bryce*, 90 n. 2

Fitzroy, Sir Almeric, *Memoirs*, 34 n. 1
Franchise (European), 23–4, 42, 45–8; (Non-European), 62–84, 86
Freeman's Journal, The, 23 n. 2

Gandhi, M. K., 32, 98
Germany, 53, 55, 93
Gladstone, Herbert (Viscount), 57
Gokhale, G. K., *Speeches*, 94
Graham, F. (Sir Frederick), 25 n. 2, 26, 27 n. 2, 43–5, 68, 69 n. 1
Great Trek, 61
Grey, Sir Edward (Visc.), 29 n 1.
Guardian, The (Manchester), 59 n. 1, 89
Guedalla, Philip, 16
Gustavus Adolphus, 86 n. 3

Haldane, R. B. (Visc.), 27; *An Autobiography*, 28 n. 1, 29 n. 1, 49 n. 2
Hardie, J. Keir, 61, 86
Headlam, C., *The Milner Papers*, 29 n. 1, 33 n. 2, 39 n. 1, 42 n. 1, 63 n. 2
Healy, Tim, 23 n. 2
Hertzog, Dr J. A. M., 63 n. 1
Hertzog, General J. B. M., 45, 49, 53, 55–6, 58
Het Volk, 24–5, 47–8
Hobhouse, Emily, 21
Hofmeyr, J. H., 36
Hungarian revolt (1956), 22 n. 3

India, 32, 54, 64, 79, 94–9
Indian National Congress, 94–6
Ireland, 23, 91, 96–9

Jameson, Dr L. S., 31, 43
Johannesburg, 20, 42, 62, 70

Keith, A. B., 25, 26 n. 1
Keppel-Jones, A. N., *When Smuts Goes*, 56 n. 2
Kitchener, Field-Marshal Lord, 23
Krüger, Professor D. W., *The Age of the Generals*, 52 n. 2; *South African Parties and Policies 1910–1960*, 55 n. 1 and 2, 58 n. 2
Kruger, Paul, 27, 40, 58, 69

INDEX

Labouchere, Henry, 40 n. 1
Labour Party, 72, 74–6, 91, 98
Language question, 31–2, 48–50, 57, 60 n. 1, 89, 96
Liberal Party, 15–16, 19–21, 23, 26–30, 33, 35–6, 40–4, 50, 55, 64–5, 67–9, 73–5, 77–8, 80–2, 90–4, 96–7, 99–100
Lloyd George, David, 16, 17 n.1, 28, 96, 97 n. 1
Lyttelton, Alfred, 74
Lyttelton Constitution, 23–4, 28, 47

Maccoby, S., *English Radicalism 1886–1914*, 41 n. 1
MacDonald, J. Ramsay, 74–5, 91 n. 3
Macmillan, H., 18, 86, 98
Magnanimity, 15, 17–18, 30, 35–6, 42, 59–60, 69, 89–90, 92–3, 96–100
Maitland, F. W., 27
Malan, Dr D. F., 58, 79, 85
Mansergh, Nicholas, *Survey of British Commonwealth Affairs 1939–52*, 50 n. 1; *Documents and Speeches on British Commonwealth Affairs 1931–52*, 53 n. 1, 79 n. 3, 82 n. 1, 83 n. 2, 84 n. 1
Marshall, Geoffrey, *Parliamentary Sovereignty and the Commonwealth*, 83 n. 1
Mehrotra, Dr S. R., 96 n. 2
Merriman, J. X., 63, 72
Millin, S. G., *General Smuts*, 16 n. 2, 93 n. 1
Milner, Alfred (Viscount), 23–4, 29 n. 1, 33, 39–40, 42, 48, 58, 62–3, 65, 90–1
Mitter, B. C., 96
Morley, John (Viscount), *Recollections*, 17 n. 2, 22 n. 2, 23 n. 1, 28 n. 1, 40 n. 1 and 2, 41, 60

Narain, Pandit Jagat, 95
Natal, 32, 35, 51–2, 63, 65, 71, 74–5, 79, 83

National Convention, 43, 49, 51–2, 72, 78–81
National Flag, 44, 54–6, 57
National (Nationalist) Party, 50, 53, 54, 56 n. 1 and 2, 80–1, 84–6
Nationalism (Afrikaner), 58–9, 99
Native Question, 28, 31–3, 36, 38, 51, 61–89, 92–4, 99–100
New York Times, The, 86 n. 1
New Zealand, 38, 79
Nicholls, G. Heaton, *South Africa in My Time*, 56 n. 1
Nokwe, Duma, 36

Observer, The, 36
Ommanney, Sir Montagu, 68
Orange River Colony (Free State), 18, 24, 25, 28, 30, 35, 36, 38, 63, 65, 66, 67, 71, 74, 75, 79, 83, 92, 95, 97

Pakistan, 79
Partition, 88
Pentland, Lord, 21
Petit, Jehangir Bamanjee, 95 n. 3
Petrie, Sir Charles, *The Life and Letters of the Rt. Hon. Sir Austen Chamberlain*, 98 n. 1
Pienaar, S. (and Anthony Sampson), *South Africa, Two Views of Separate Development*, 87 n. 1
Population, 31–2, 39–40, 45–7, 59
Predikants, 44–5, 48
Pretoria, 30, 58, 61
Progressive Association, 47
Protectorates (High Commission Territories), 78–80, 88
Pyrah, G. B., *Imperial Policy and South Africa 1902–10*, 21 n. 3

Redmond, John, 96, 97 n. 1, 98
Referendum (on Republic), 58–9
Republic (South African), 44–5, 50, 53–4, 56–9, 80, 85, 87, 100
Republics, Boer, 16–18, 20, 23, 27–9, 31, 38, 45, 57, 61–4, 90–1, 94, 96, 97
Responsible Government Association, 24, 25 n. 1, 47, 70–1

Responsible self-government, 17–20, 23–31, 33, 36, 38–9, 43, 45–6, 48, 54, 68–9, 71, 77, 87, 91, 93–7

Rhodes, Cecil J., 40 n. 1, 62

Riddell, Lord, *More Pages from My Diary*, 17 n. 1

Roberts, M. (and A. E. G. Trollip), *The South African Opposition 1939–45*, 57 n. 1

Rolland, Romain, 32; *Mahatma Gandhi*, 32 n. 2

Rosebery, 5th Earl of, 20, 29 n. 1

Schreiner, W. P., 71–2, 76

Seely, Colonel J. E. B., 91

Selborne, 2nd Earl of, 20, 24, 35, 44–5, 46 n. 4, 47 n. 1, 48, 49 n. 1, 58, 65–7, 69 n. 1, 70, 71 n. 1 and 2, 72, 77 n. 1, 78 n. 1 and 2, 79 n. 2, 81 n. 2, 94 n. 1

Senate, 81, 84, 86

Senate Act (1955), 81 n. 1

Senate Act (1960), 81 n. 1

Separate Representation of Voters' Act (1951), 82–3

Sharpeville, 16

Smith, F. E. (1st Earl of Birkenhead), 97

Smith, Goldwin, 90

Smuts, General J. C., 15–16, 23, 25–7, 30, 43–6, 51–3, 56, 58, 72, 93, 97–9

South Africa Act (1909), 15–16, 35–6, 49, 52, 73–7, 79–80, 82–4, 91–2

South African Citizenship Act (1949), 57

South African Native Convention, 93–4

South African Temperance Alliance, 85

South African War (1899–1902), 15, 20, 27, 29–30, 34, 41, 44, 58, 60, 62–4, 90–1, 94

Spender, J. A., *Life of the Right Hon. Sir Henry Campbell-Bannerman*, 19 n. 1, 20 n. 2, 21 n. 1 and 3, 22 n. 1 and 3, 30 n. 1, 31 n. 1, 41 n. 3; (and C. Asquith), *Life of Lord Oxford and Asquith*, 20 n. 1, 37 n. 1

Status of the Union Act (1934), 53, 75, 82

Statute of Westminster (1931), 18, 81–4

Strijdom, J. G., 53–6, 86

Supreme Court, 83–4

Swaziland, 78–80

Thompson, Professor L. M., *The Unification of South Africa 1902–1910*, 35, 52 n. 1, 59 n. 3, 63 n. 3, 72 n. 2, 73

Times, The, 17, 29–30, 40 n. 1 and 2, 41 n. 1, 56 n. 3, 58 n. 1, 59 n. 2, 63 n. 1

Transvaal, 18–20, 24–8, 30–1, 35–6, 38–9, 43–9, 51–2, 58 n. 1, 62–3, 65–7, 69–72, 74–5, 77–9, 83, 92–3, 95, 97

Transvaler, Die, 50

Two nation theory, 87

Union (in South Africa), 16–17, 20, 33–6, 47, 51–2, 59, 71–8, 87

Union of South Africa, The, 15, 18, 31, 35–7, 52–4, 57, 76, 78–9, 81–90, 92, 94–5, 98–9

Unionist Party, 18, 22–4, 40, 42, 65, 71, 73, 91, 97

United Party, 56

Van den Heever, C. M., *General J. B. M. Hertzog*, 45 n. 2

Van Heerden, W., 59 n. 1

Vereeniging, Treaty of (1902), 15–16, 23–6, 42, 64–5, 67, 69, 76–8, 91

Verwoerd, Dr Hendrik, 58–9, 63

Wade, Professor E. C. S., 83 n. 1

Walker, E. A., *Lord de Villiers and His Times*, 43 n. 1; *W. P. Schreiner, A South African*, 72 n. 4

Wernher, Julius, 39

West Ridgeway Committee, 43, 47, 67–8

West Ridgeway, Sir Joseph, 47

For Product Safety Concerns and Information please contact our EU representative GPSR@taylorandfrancis.com
Taylor & Francis Verlag GmbH, Kaufingerstraße 24, 80331 München, Germany

www.ingramcontent.com/pod-product-compliance
Lightning Source LLC
Chambersburg PA
CBHW070543300426
44113CB00011B/1769